Pam, I hope you choose HAPPY!

Be Happy by Choice

MARK EIGLARSH

Wonderful meeting you!

Best

Be Happy by Choice

MARK EIGLARSH

Editing by Kyle Ashcraft and Dave Bricker

Book layout by Dave Bricker

Cover design by Anastasia Ziemba

ISBN: 978-1-7340695-0-1

*For my extraordinary wife Beth and our
amazing children Evan, Julia and Owen.
I will forever love you unconditionally.*

Contents

INTRODUCTION

I never dreamt I'd be writing a book about happiness; lawyers aren't known to be the happiest people in the world (I have, however, heard many other choice words used to describe us). I definitely wasn't "happy" before. Truth be told, I was the opposite. It wasn't that I was *unhappy;* it's just that my moods would fluctuate. I'd be happy one minute and then something would happen that would alter how I felt. I allowed external forces to dictate how I felt.

Even when I started realizing how erratic my moods were and that my happiness was short-lived and sporadic, I did little to change. I was a loud guy who erroneously thought the spiritual arena was made up of hokey, flakey malarkey.

I'd come to learn how little I knew and how off my perspective was.

It wasn't until the pain grew that I became open to change. From that openness came exposure to infinite tools, ideas, speakers, formulas, you name it. I launched headfirst into this journey and reached out for anything that would alter my way of thinking. I thought I would end up proving to myself, *You see? All this effort and nothing happened. Such crap! What a colossal waste of time!*

But a crazy thing happened after I put forth the effort and explored solutions: *I started to get better.* I became happier. By holding onto the information I liked and spitting out the rest, I began to assemble my own formula for happiness. After solidifying my happiness formula, I tried it out on my most important client — me — and it worked!

I'm not suggesting I'm happy around the clock. I'm a human, living in the real world. I don't spend my days wrapped in a toga with my legs crossed in deep meditation, perched on top of a mountain in Bhutan. As a litigator, I spend most days in court fighting for my clients. Because of what I do, I face immense challenges on a daily basis. That's why I turn to my formula. The more I do, the better I feel. The more intentionally I embrace my formula, the better the results. And of course, the converse is true.

It took me a while to write this book. *Who the hell am I to write a spiritual book about happiness? That type of thing is reserved for guru types.* What clothed itself as rational thinking was my insecurities trying to prevent me from being of service. But I've got something special to share. Helping others helps me.

I'm not telling you to be happy. That decision is up to you; no one is forcing you. In the past, I chose to be miserable; few things could have gotten me to change. But if you *do* want to be happy, this book offers a useful formula and the tools you need.

I am not a doctor, psychologist or behavioral therapist. What works for me may not work for everyone. Some people suffer from clinical depression and/or other mental illnesses. This book is not a substitute for a mental health professional.

Many reading my "victim story" will have gone through much worse. I'm not suggesting I've had it that rough. I've gone through challenges, but so has everyone else. Pain is inevitable but suffering is optional!

ACKNOWLEDGMENTS

I am grateful to so many people for making this book possible. I thank all those whose actions caused me pain. Without your efforts, I would never have longed for a better way of feeling and thinking. For every time you cut me off in traffic, said unkind things to me, or tried to hurt me, thank you. I am as grateful to you as I am to those who treated me well. Without experiencing your darkness, I could have never begun to appreciate the light.

To those authors and speakers who influenced me so greatly, your words lifted me up and inspired me during the most challenging of days. The list is long, so to name a few, thanks to Deepak Chopra, Eckhart Tolle, Don Miguel Ruiz, Shawn Achor, and Tony Robbins. I especially want to acknowledge Mo Gawdat for his teachings and his spectacular book, *Solve for Happy.* Your wisdom and words changed my life.

I'm extremely grateful to my friends and family who supported me and showed me unconditional love as I wrote this book. I want to specifically thank: Dorothy Eiglarsh, Larry "Happy" Eiglarsh,

Bruce Turkel, Gary Aniraf, Terry Pappy, Yani Antelo, Brad Meltzer, Megyn Kelly, Dr. Drew Pinsky, Melissa Byers, Caroline De Posada, David Schweiger, Mitch Feldman, Robert Coppel, Manny Munoz, Jimmy Cefalo, Scott Sarbey, Brent Spechler, Elissa Holder, Adam Herman, Jen Herman, Scott Krasick, Bryan Glazer, Cari Buddman, Jessica Buddman, Kristen Odijk, Dan Lurvey, Honit Simon, Jenny Levinson, and Adam Eisner. I could write an entire book solely about my extraordinary wife Beth who has been the perfect life partner for me. We have three wonderful children to whom I am also extremely grateful. Thank you, my dear Evan, Julia and Owen. I am so grateful to be your dad.

While this process of learning happiness hasn't been easy, it's been fulfilling and therapeutic. My heart is filled with love and gratitude.

1

MY VICTIM STORY

While I never took steps to take my own life, I remember thinking one day on my way to court, *If I were to die in a car crash, at least my pain would finally go away.* The emotional pain I had been carrying for months was so intense that I found myself thinking and acting in ways that frightened me. I had never experienced that kind of darkness. It seeped into my heart and head, breaking every part of me. Even breathing became a challenge.

Broken and deflated, I was convinced that FAILURE was written in all caps across my forehead with a bold Sharpie. My marriage, which I treasured, was threatened. We were miserable. Loving and effortless communication had been replaced by shouting matches fueled by bouts of anger. While I tried to be strong for my three young children, I found it difficult because of the dark place I was in. My fits of anger even frightened *me.*

On those rare occasions when I was able to view my life from an outsider's perspective, I knew I needed to change, but I had no clue where to begin. I didn't have any tools. I was looking for a corner in a round room. *How the hell did I get to this point?*

Things hadn't always been that way. For years, I had the perfect marriage. The way my wife and I met seemed to be the result of divine intervention. Standing in the buffet line at a fundraiser held at the Fontainebleau Miami Beach Hotel in January 1999, I found myself puzzled over the food choices. *Baked ziti and potato pancakes?* They just didn't seem to go together.

As I pondered this odd pairing, I looked up and saw Beth amidst a crowd of 1,700 people. I was blown away. She was beautiful, petite, sexy, and energetic. During our brief conversation, she looked at my name tag and asked if I had twin sisters. I was stunned. She told me that she had met my twin sisters Jenny and Ruth in Israel during a summer semester abroad at the Alexander Muss High School in Israel program fifteen years before.

Taken aback by our encounter, I called one of my sisters and excitedly asked Jenny, "Remember a girl named Beth Andron…? Petite, adorable, big boobs?"

"Yeah, what about her?" my sister responded.

"Well, what do you think of her?"

"She was fine..," she paused and then continued sarcastically, "But Mark, that was fifteen years ago!"

I realized how silly my call was.

Our first date, which was meant to last long enough to drink a cup of coffee, ended up being an eleven-hour marathon. We couldn't get enough of each other. I proposed to her ten months later with a poem called, "You Complete Me." We were married ten months after that.

In the swirl of new love, we laughed and enjoyed seamless communication. We were living a fairytale.

We had much in common due to our similar upbringings. Like my wife, I was born in 1968. While she was born in North Miami, Florida, I was born in Miami Beach, fifteen minutes south. Like her, I enjoyed what I considered to be a happy childhood. My mother was a teacher and my father was a pharmacist. He owned a drug store on Miami Beach and hated what he did for a living.

We were "Conservative Jews," which meant we weren't Orthodox (the most religious) nor were we Reform (the least). We went to temple, primarily for special events and Jewish holidays.

As a boy, I attended Hebrew school, which I despised. I always viewed religion as something that had been forced upon me by my parents. They used guilt and fear to make me connect to the religion and buy into the Jewish activities they wanted me to participate in. I asked them about the traditions and practices of our religion, but their answers never left me satisfied. I sensed that was what their parents had done, and that's what was expected of us. I had little emotional connection to the religion and no spiritual connection to a Higher Power.

One day, something changed. Beth and I were overjoyed to find out we were pregnant. The excitement we felt made our relationship even more perfect. Every night I would kiss her belly before we went to sleep, wanting to connect with our unborn child.

When we went in for a routine sonogram about halfway through our pregnancy, our only concern was whether the doctor would screw up and reveal the sex of the baby. We wanted that to be a surprise.

We were informed of something far worse. During this visit, we heard the word *Encephalocele* for the first time. The doctor told us our son had an extremely rare neural tube defect characterized by the brain protruding through an opening in the skull. The joy we had felt for the past five months twisted into crushing pain as we were told we would have to terminate the twenty-week pregnancy. There were no other options. We were told that our baby wouldn't survive outside of the womb. To make matters worse, we were forced to wait a week to have the procedure because our obstetrician was on vacation.

Lying in bed with our dying son in her womb, my wife looked delicate and afraid. I tried offsetting this enormous agony by being a source of light, by tossing her snippets of Tony Robbins philosophy without allowing her to grieve the way she needed to.

The procedure itself was unspeakably horrific — clinical and heartless. Having never had a child, I didn't realize what we had lost. I also didn't comprehend what a devastating loss this was for Beth. Hopelessness poured through her. To manage our pain, I was determined to be positive, and I thereby nullified the pain we both felt. On top of failing to sympathize with my wife's feelings, my judgment made her feel bad for feeling bad. *Why can't she just move on?* I wondered. *Why on Earth is she choosing victimhood over triumph? We can always have more children.*

I didn't comprehend the way she needed to process this horrible experience. The contrast between how we handled our grief sparked resentful feelings, but due to my solution-oriented mindset, I kept searching for a way out of the pain.

One evening when I came home from work, I grabbed Beth's hand and instructed her to close her eyes and promise not to open them. She resisted at first, but I ran to the other room and returned with something in my hands that I viewed as the solution to our problems.

"Open your eyes!"

She screamed with excitement and began to smile so enthusiastically that I was shaken. I hadn't seen that smile on my Beth's face in quite some time. The instant high I felt as I watched her beam with joy was sensational.

The "object" was a yellow Labrador Retriever puppy.

A cuter dog you could not find. We named her "Starr" (because one "r" was simply not enough for Beth). We redirected the love and energy we could no longer share with our dead son to this new four-legged family member. We were so absorbed with Starr that we didn't even mind the havoc she was wreaking across our newly renovated home.

Life improved … for a while.

One day, while eating breakfast, I watched Starr, who was two weeks shy of her first birthday, joyfully devour a softball that had made its way into our yard. *Wow, look how happy she is. Dogs have it made. I wish I were as happy as my sweet dog.* Starr seemed fine for most of that day, and even during our morning run. But late in the afternoon, my wife called and insisted we take Starr to the vet because she was acting abnormally. Fearing exorbitant vet bills and assuming our dog was probably fine, I was reluctant to support the vet visit.

I spoke with the vet a few hours later. Starr needed immediate surgery due to the internal damage from portions of the softball attempting to make their way through her digestive system.

Immediately after surgery, I received the call from our vet telling me that our dear Starr had died. I was *shocked*. Before I could begin to process the dreadful news, Beth walked in the front door. I'll never forget that moment. She let out howling screams and sobbed frantically.

Our former grief came roaring back. The feeling of losing our son had never left us, and that pain was multiplied by losing our dog just a year later.

Again, each of us handled the loss differently. I tried using the same ineffective approach as before to console her. I was judgmental and controlling; I didn't allow her the time and space to grieve the way she needed to.

Grief is a process. If you don't allow for feelings of loss, they *will* express themselves in unhealthy ways. What you suppress will not disappear. For a time, we pretended to move on, allowing our daily routine to fill the void in our hearts. Within a period of five years, we had three healthy children, but the demands of raising small kids while still carrying around unprocessed feelings from our first pregnancy pushed Beth and me over the edge. We went through numerous other significant trials and tribulations.

Our personal challenges left me a mess. We were angry, frustrated, sad, lonely, and fearful. Resentment started to build; I began to feel extremely hurt. We were emotional wrecks. Intimacy of any sort was rare, which only fed my neediness and insecurity. Depression seeped through the crevices of my psyche. I kept my darkest feelings hidden from the world at a time when I most needed to express them. I just couldn't talk about them; I was embarrassed to feel so weak. Anger replaced joy and tears replaced laughter. Sadness filled our home. I felt like a failure; nothing seemed to make a difference. If nothing changed, it would mean the end of our marriage.

Working every day was challenging under that emotional burden. My clients — some of whom were in jail — seemed happier than I was. They were in a physical prison, but I was in an emotional one. And I didn't realize that I was the one who had put myself there.

My mood was led by my circumstances. If a judge or jury ruled in my favor, I was happy. If a prosecutor gave me the plea-bargain I had fought for, I was happy. If I didn't get what I wanted, I felt dejected. If a judge treated me poorly, it threw me off for the rest of the day. Moments of joy caused by positive outcomes were immediately replaced by anger and pain.

If someone cut me off in traffic, I felt they were disrespecting me. I actually believed that whatever inappropriate move they made with their car was specifically done against me. I became offended at the drop of a hat, believing everyone was out to get the best of me. I would shift into rage mode and surrender leadership of myself, just long enough to speed up alongside them and give them the middle finger. I'd love to be able to say my kids were never in my car when I acted that way, but that wouldn't be accurate. My road-rage jeopardized my life and the lives of those around me.

One low point took place when I was leaving a local gas station. A woman was frantically trying to catch my attention, and I ignored her; I was trying to avoid human contact as much as possible. Her gestures became more pronounced, making her impossible to ignore. She yelled, "The thing! The thing!" while pointing at the side of my car.

I reluctantly rolled down my car window. *"What?"*

She pointed at the gas tank opening on my vehicle. "Look!"

I had begun driving away from the gas pump with the nozzle still in my car, fully disconnecting the hose from the pump. Instead of thanking her like a normal, grateful person would have done, I snarled, "You couldn't have told me sooner?" I was too lost in thought over how much reattaching the nozzle to the pump was going to cost to actually be appreciative.

But in that moment, my dark behavior scared me. *Who have I become?* My behavior was intolerable. I had hit bottom.

Action Steps

1. Write out your "victim story." Be extremely detailed while documenting your challenges. Has someone emotionally or physically hurt you in the past? Write it all down. Don't leave anything out. Start with your earliest childhood memories and keep going until you get to the present.

2. Are you willing to forgive those who wronged you? Write letters of forgiveness with the reason(s) why. Forgiveness doesn't mean you forget or condone the behavior; it just means you will no longer allow it to control or adversely affect your life. You don't have to send the letters; writing them is the important part.

2

THE ROAD TO RECOVERY

Excruciating pain motivated me to want to change.

What's the most effective way to achieve a different outcome? *By trying something different.* I resolved to *pretend* my way out of my misery, even if that only gave me a fraction of a chance. Once I chose to let go and get out of my own way, I began to realize the benefits of my efforts.

I tried everything I could find that might put me on the path toward serenity. If I found a book with the word *happy* in the title, I read it. If a meeting, speaker, workshop, podcast, seminar, or retreat promised to teach me to be happier, I was all over it.

Some strategies were helpful and worth the time; others, not so much. My approach was to experience it all, taking away what was helpful and leaving the rest. I loved being at the Deepak Chopra Wellness Center in Carlsbad, California. Talk about the "sweet spot of the universe." Learning about meditation, healthy eating, and healthy thinking served me well. However, colon cleanses — "spiritual enemas" — left me feeling uncomfortable and confused. But I took what I liked from the experience and left the rest, chewing the meat and spitting out the bones.

Beth became knee-deep in her own spiritual recovery. We attended spiritual retreats together and found most of the activities to be beneficial. At one retreat, she suggested we should "paint on a horse." I thought she had lost her mind. I pictured us trying to steady the paintbrush on a canvas while "Trigger" moved anxiously from side to side.

"No, silly. When I say 'paint on a horse,' I mean we'll be painting *onto* a horse. We get to use the horse as a living canvas."

Now I was sure she had lost her mind. *Why the hell would we do that?*

A few months later we were actually smearing paint across a horse's body. It was surprisingly therapeutic, and the horse didn't seem to mind.

The more I did, the more results I saw. The more meditation, reading, and service I embraced, the better I felt.

As the years went by, I accumulated experiences, principles, and ideas. As I learned to be of service, I realized I had something to offer that would help others. Writing a book would serve as an effective tool for accomplishing that. I would make my process as helpful to those who read about my journey as it was to me.

I had reservations: I was concerned about what my extraordinary wife might think. Going public with the painful details of my "victim story" meant revealing personal and painful memories. I told Beth I wouldn't publish the book without her blessing.

Because she also lives a life of service, Beth understands the importance of this book. Our marriage is stronger today than it has ever been because of what we experienced individually and collectively. We turned every conflict into growing opportunities.

Certain thoughts held me back: *Who am I to write a book? Writing a book to help people achieve and maintain happiness is for 'spiritual gurus,' not for South Florida trial lawyers.*

I chose to change those thoughts. The shift came unexpectedly at a random moment on a flight home from Dallas to Fort Lauderdale. Everything I had learned and wanted to share with others came together in one step-by-step formula. I knew I had something special that could transform lives.

Nothing could stop me from sharing it with the world.

Setting Up the Solution

Thoughts, feelings, actions: three important words that will change your life. Our thoughts dictate our feelings, and our feelings dictate our actions. If we think negative thoughts — thoughts that don't serve us well — we feel terrible. This manifests itself in our behavior and how we carry ourselves. When that happens, we find ourselves attracting what we don't want. When we think positively by choosing thoughts that do serve us well, we feel great and act accordingly. This attracts the wonderful gifts we deserve. The key to happiness then, is to focus on our thoughts and develop tools that help us change our "stinkin' thinkin.'"

Many thoughts *don't* serve us well. We all have them: *I'm not smart enough, pretty enough, handsome enough, thin enough, rich enough, successful enough, etc. My wife/life/job/boyfriend sucks! I wish life were different!* As if these thoughts about our own lives weren't hurtful enough, we experience negative thoughts about others: *He's a jerk. She's a horrible person. I want to kill him. He's out for me.* None of these harmful thoughts serve us well; all they do is bring us down.

Pause and write down your negative thoughts. Don't rush. Take your time and allow them to flow out of you onto paper. These thoughts can be about the past, present, or future. Identify them all. Take breaks from this assignment as needed to ensure you've been thorough. One thought will often lead to a string of others so dig deep and delve into every thought that doesn't serve you. This exercise will stir up emotions of insecurity, hurt, and guilt, but press on. After you implement the happiness formula, you will feel better.

Skeptical? Good!

Perhaps you're wondering, *What's with all this happiness crap? Does it really matter if I'm happy? I just want to make a lot of money and be successful, and then I'll be happy naturally.*

A skeptic is "a person inclined to question or doubt accepted opinions." Synonyms include, "cynic," "doubter," "questioner," and "scoffer." Any of those nouns could be replaced with "*Mark*." That's still me, even after my "spiritual awakening."

This mindset is a blessing and a curse. It makes things difficult to accept, which helps me thrive as a trial lawyer. By rejecting things that don't help my client or myself, I am empowered to search further and deeper to uncover the truth — which isn't always what prosecutors are trying to feed me. I have a gift for creating reasonable doubt even when the evidence against my client seems convincing. These skills are essential when defending a criminal case.

But this attitude doesn't always serve us well in our personal lives. By questioning and doubting everything, we prevent ourselves from growing. Instead of embracing beneficial principles and beliefs, we reject what we read or hear. Only by thinking matters through and choosing to be open to new thoughts and ideas will you be able to make major shifts.

Statistics from a *Harvard Business Review* study[1] reveal the value of happiness in the workplace. Happy employees:

- Produce 37% greater sales
- Are 31% more productive
- Suffer 23% fewer fatigue symptoms
- Are 300% more creative

For personal and professional reasons, happiness makes a scientifically measurable difference. Happiness makes good common sense and good business sense. The happier my employees are, the more productive they are, which benefits everyone — and the same goes for me.

Pursuing happiness for practical reasons or because it feels better than the alternative is simply a sensible thing to do.

As you consider the principles in this book, engage your critical, skeptical mind — but not to the point where you dismiss useful ideas and practices out-of-hand. The suggested strategies for finding happiness work whether you believe in them or not. Give the exercises a try. If you're like me, your inner skeptic may wind up wondering how and why they work when you were so sure they wouldn't. That's a good problem to have.

---

1   https://hbr.org/2011/06/the-happiness-dividend

What is happiness?

Defining happiness isn't easy. If you were to ask a hundred people what happiness means, you would get a hundred different definitions.

Webster's Dictionary defines "happiness" as "the quality or state of being happy."

Huh? What's the definition of "happy?"

There's an answer for that, too. "Happy" means, "delighted, pleased, or glad."

Other dictionary definitions include, "Good fortune, pleasure, contentment, and joy."

United States Supreme Court Justice Potter Stewart must have felt equal frustration when trying to define "obscenity." In the 1964 landmark case of *Jacobellis v. Ohio,* while explaining why certain material was constitutionally protected and not obscene, Stewart wrote, "I know it when I see it."

That's as close as you'll get to defining "happiness": You know it when you see it. You also know it when you *feel* it.

Let's define "happiness" as "the result of choosing thoughts that serve you well." That's probably not the definition you were expecting, but it took many years to come to that understanding. When we choose thoughts that serve us well, we feel happy, free, serene, and joyful. When we embrace thoughts that don't serve us well, we become unhappy, and even miserable or depressed.

You have the choice to either adopt or reject the thoughts your brain sends your way. That choice has a pronounced impact on your physical and emotional well-being. In light of the colossal importance of selecting thoughts wisely, and given how difficult it can be to choose our thoughts instead of allowing them to choose themselves, I offer a formula. The rest of this book is dedicated to that formula.

Don't rush through these chapters like you would your favorite action novel. Read a section, pause to process it, and consider how you can apply it. Take the time you need to soak in each step, allow it to alter the way you think, and experience real, positive change. Also, don't just *consider* working the exercises at the end of each chapter. Take the time to *do* them wholeheartedly and zealously. The more committed you are, the more change you'll achieve.

Action Steps

1. What is your definition of happiness?

2. Why do you deserve to be happier?

3. In great detail, list your thoughts that do not serve you well.

3

RECLAIM YOUR HAPPINESS

Introduction to the Formula

Any time you feel an unwanted emotion, you are most likely embracing thoughts that do not serve you well — what I call, "stinkin' thinkin.'" When that occurs, think of SALADS! That's right; the key to your current and future happiness can be found in SALADS! I am not suggesting that if you eat salads, you will turn your frown upside down (although adding more healthy salads to your diet wouldn't be a bad idea). SALADS is an acronym; each letter represents one step in the happiness formula.

Action Steps

Which of these feelings do you experience regularly?
    Sadness, loneliness, envy, depression, anxiety, anger, ner-
    vousness, fear, annoyance, guilt, judgment, disappointment,

despair, frustration, discouragement, shame, hate, unloved, bitterness, victimized, disillusioned, wronged, rejected, pained, miserable, offended, heartbroken, empty or scared.

Which of those feelings do you wish you didn't feel regularly?

What other feelings do you wish you didn't feel regularly?

STEP 1: STOP!

The first "S" in SALADS stands for "Stop!" Whenever you feel an emotion you no longer wish to feel, *stop!* Whether you're sad, lonely, envious, depressed, anxious, angry, nervous, fearful, annoyed, guilty, judgmental, disappointed, despairing, frustrated, discouraged, ashamed, hateful, unloved, bitter, victimized, disillusioned, wronged, rejected, pained, miserable, offended, heartbroken, empty, or scared, the key to changing negative emotions is to determine whether you actually *want* to feel different.

Why would anyone *want* to feel nervous?"

Some believe that feeling nervous or stressed will motivate them to study harder for a test or prepare more earnestly for their upcoming project.

Why would anyone *choose* to feel sad?

Many choose to allocate a period of time to be in touch with their sadness during a grieving process. Choosing happiness prematurely hinders what many people need to feel and go through to effectively process loss.

Many of us become accustomed to feeling the same way every day; we become, well, emotionally attached to our emotions. If you hold onto feeling hopeless for 300 days, and suddenly choose on day 301 to let go of your hopelessness and reach out for purpose, you will probably feel uncomfortable because you are opening yourself up to new emotions. The global spiritual leader, Thich Nhat Hanh, summed this struggle up perfectly: "People have a hard time letting go of their suffering. Out of fear of the unknown, they prefer suffering that is familiar."

If comfort is our goal, we will never experience an emotional breakthrough.

Be clear: It's okay to choose to feel however you like. Sadness and unhappiness, for example, are normal emotions. The only people who don't have feelings are psychopaths and the dead. Since you're definitely not the latter and hopefully not the former, give yourself permission to feel however you'd like. I'm not telling you *to* change how you feel; I'm merely informing you that you have the power to *choose* how you feel.

When you feel emotions that don't serve you well, *stop*. Don't skip to step two or do anything else until you've stopped. Most often, it's not in your best interest to react from a negative state.

Imagine you're in traffic and someone cuts you off. Typically, you feel a swell of a thousand emotions, none of which serve you well. You become filled with anger, convinced that the other driver did this to you with the sole intent of ruining your day. Or maybe you feel disrespected, frustrated, victimized or offended. You cannot trust yourself to make the most rational decisions in these heated moments.

When someone cut me off, I would transform from calm to *steaming* unless I received an apologetic gesture from the other driver. Rarely did I receive such a gesture, and rarely did I make the choice to mentally stop. I reacted in a way that didn't serve me or my passengers well. I would speed up and give the other driver a gesture I thought they deserved.

Immediately after engaging in that behavior, I would feel ashamed and even more unhappy.

Stop doesn't only apply to stories of road rage. If a boss, spouse, friend, relative, co-worker, girlfriend, or boyfriend, says or does something that stirs unwanted emotions within you, just *stop*. 98% of the time, your initial reaction will not serve either of you well. Losing control around someone you know is even more harmful than with a stranger; the residue of hurt emotions takes a long time to wash away.

The words that flow from our lips and the actions we exhibit when affected by anger or anxiety are almost never the ideal way to respond.

Just stop.

Reminder 1: BREATHE

After you stop, take a deep breath. Now do it again. Breathe through your nose, fill your lungs with air, and then exhale through your mouth. Studies[2] have shown that deep breathing improves your mental and physical health. Deep breathing can reduce stress and buy you time to think of what to do next. Taking a breath when you feel any emotion that doesn't serve you well will make the difference between a healthy response and an out-of-control reaction.

When breathing, try the "3 x 3 method," designed by marriage and family therapist Phil Boissiere. In his 2017 Ted Talk,[3] Boissiere explains that the first step is to name a physical object around you (e.g. "That's a lamp"). Then take a deep breath by inhaling slowly and then exhaling slowly. Find and name another object and repeat the process, taking deep breaths, slowly in and slowly out. Repeating this process three times will change how you feel by helping you become more mindful of your situation.

The Time I Failed to Breathe

My client was facing a life sentence for burglary with assault and armed robbery. She had been a prostitute most of her life,

---

2   https://www.health.harvard.edu/mind-and-mood/relaxation-techniques-breath-control-helps-quell-errant-stress-response
3   https://www.youtube.com/watch?v=ad7HqXEc2Sc

and based on her extensive criminal record, she was labeled a "habitual violent offender" by the prosecutors. These charges stemmed from an incident in which she and a friend had allegedly entered her client's house and held a machete to his throat while her accomplice took his wallet. She could have gotten a life sentence for this.

I was excited and a little nervous about going to trial because we would be before the infamous Judge Ellen "Maximum" Morphonios. Having been featured in stories by *60 Minutes* and *People Magazine*, Judge Morphonios was known for dishing out thousand-year sentences. She was also known for bizarre behavior. After sentencing a rapist to a life sentence, she reportedly stood up, lifted her robe to reveal her shapely legs, and remarked, "That's the last time in your life that you're going to see a pair of legs like this."

Another story involved a defendant's mother who cried so hard that she passed out on the floor. Morphonios continued the court's business as if nothing had happened. "Next defendant! Step forward. Step over the body."

It was evident that the judge had taken a liking to the victim, who was in his late 90s.

Testifying through a Spanish interpreter, the victim revealed that he had been paying for sexual services from my client, three times a week for several years. They had engaged, he said, in both oral and regular sex. Judge Morphonios appeared astonished and envious.

Her eyes popping in disbelief, she interrupted the prosecutor's questioning and, in her booming southern accent, asked the victim, "Sir, what do you eat for breakfast?"

"Cuban toast," he answered.

"Well, then I got to get me some Cuban toast," she said.

The victim testified that his last encounter with my client had been very different. After he had opened the door to his home, the defendant and her female friend had forcibly pushed their way inside, he claimed. According to him, my client had grabbed the victim's machete and held it to his neck while the co-defendant removed the victim's wallet, which contained only a few dollars.

During the victim's testimony, the veteran prosecutor ran into a problem. When she asked the elderly victim how he had felt with a machete at his throat, he gave only a one-word response. In Spanish, it sounded like "ee-mah-hee-neh," which was translated as, "imagine." Realizing that this response would be insufficient to establish on the record that he had been in a state of fear, she persisted. "Sir, were you scared when the defendant held the machete at your throat?" With passion, the victim repeated his original response: "Ee-mah-hee-neh."

Despite my strenuous objections to staying focused on one question for so long, the judge continued to allow the prosecutor to try leading the witness into saying he was scared. Finally, the impatient judge intervened; she not only put up with the prosecutor's insistence, she contributed to it!

"Let me give this a try," she told the prosecutor. I was caught in a game of "tag-team prosecution." The judge turned to the victim and said, "Sir, you must have been petrified when she put the machete to your throat."

I vehemently objected to putting words in the victim's mouth. I was outraged. The judge had forgotten her oath of impartiality, and had joined forces with the prosecutor to help her case. The only person in the room whom the jurors trusted had assumed the role of prosecutor. What a gut punch! Of all the things I had foreseen happening in this case, I had never envisioned this.

The judge refused to stop. "Sir, when she put that machete to your throat, you must have had the fear of God in you."

All she could elicit was an increasingly vehement "Ee-mah-hee-neh."

I was livid.

The judge kept overruling my numerous objections concerning her improper conduct. Feeling out of control, I felt a tightness in my chest. I needed to breathe, but didn't. *I was losing it.* What the judge was doing was incredibly improper, something I had never seen a judge do before. Emotional, I chose to react in the moment. I forgot about the many spiritual tools I had at my disposal. What I needed to help me deal with this judge gone wild was a big deep breath. Had I simply taken that deep breath, I would have realized that the judge's behavior was so out of line that the appellate court would surely reverse any ruling against my client. I let my thoughts and emotions blind me.

The judge gave up on the witness and turned to the jury: "I'm making a finding that any reasonable person, upon having a machete at their throat, would be afraid." This was the most egregious breach of judicial conduct I have ever witnessed. I lost it.

Because I had failed to take a deep breath, the scene tumbled downhill. We went back and forth. I told her that such partiality from a judge was unacceptable. She told me to back down. The way she responded to my over-the-top objections showed the jurors that the judge was against me. As a trial lawyer, that's the last thing you want to see happen. Letting my emotions run rampant likely hindered my ability to win the case.

Fortunately, the Third District Court of Appeal threw out my client's conviction and remanded the case for retrial. "The judge's comments unduly prejudiced the jury against the defendant," the appellate court said. As time dragged on, the case against my client grew weaker; the victim became older, sicker, and less mentally coherent. As a result, the prosecutor offered my client a plea bargain of six years in prison with full credit for time already served. A short time later she was out, courtesy of the eccentric judge.

When stressful moments happen take a deep breath. Tell yourself, "This will all work out." Go a step further and envision an outcome that is even better than you could rationally hope for. It all starts with one deep breath.

Reminder 2: "Just You!"

After you stop and breathe, focus on two simple words: "Just You!" (These words are stamped on my personalized Florida license plate.) When you say these two words, you affirm that the sole person responsible for your happiness is — you!

When I was a child, I depended on my parents, schoolteachers, friends, and relatives to bring me happiness. Later, when I started dating, I depended on various women to bring me happiness. Once I got married, I believed it was my wife's responsibility to make me happy.

I bought into the "Maguire Myth," which is based on the movie, *Jerry Maguire.* With tears in his eyes, Tom Cruise's character pours his heart out to Renée Zellweger's character, "You complete me."

I have since come to learn that my wife and I do not complete each other; we are each complete. We don't need each other to make us happy; we must each be happy individuals on our own if we are to be a happy couple.

I am a much better person with Beth in my life. I am happier with her as my life partner, my best friend, and the one whom I love unconditionally. However, my dependency upon my wife and others for happiness had to end.

One subject they never teach in school is how to develop tools to create happiness from the inside. Once I began to focus on myself — on *just you!* — I started channeling my energy into the one, and only one, I should count on for unconditional love and happiness.

Embracing this concept will empower you. You will realize that the decades you spent trying to manipulate others into giving you happiness are over. All that energy can be targeted toward creating happiness for the only one you can control — yourself — *just you.* You may think it sounds selfish, but it's not. Consider it self-love. If you aren't going to take care of yourself, who will?

Reminder 3: We Were All Born Happy

Something that happened since your birth is blocking you from feeling the happiness that once belonged to you. Did you do anything to earn the happiness you possessed when you exited your mother's womb? No; it was just part of how we were designed, an innate feature of being human. You don't have to go searching for this elusive thing called "happiness." It's like searching frantically for your keys and then discovering they've been in your hand all along. Happiness has been in you since the day you were born. You can find this happiness once again by tearing down the barriers.

Consider the life of a toddler. As long as their basic needs are met — a clean diaper, a full belly, and a sufficiently cozy environment — they are as happy as can be. It's only when we get older and take on thoughts that don't serve us well that we start to deny ourselves the happiness we fully deserve.

Thoughts connected to the past and the future interfere with our birthright happiness. We let negative experiences from the past flood into the present because we fear they will re-materialize in the future. If my dad yelled at me when I was ten years old, when I am 30, I may fear that my boss will yell at me. Once we identify these patterns, we can begin to recognize how irrational they are.

When I Failed to Stop — Miguel Macias's Story

Even though I've developed a life-changing formula for reclaiming one's happiness and I use it daily, I'm not perfect; I still have my days. Because I'm human, I continue to fall into behavior that doesn't serve me well. These days, I just do it less frequently and I transition rapidly back to happiness with minimal effort.

The following story illustrates how I failed to stop when I should have and shares the adverse consequences that followed.

I was contacted by the parents of twenty-year-old Miguel Macias, a handyman from Homestead, Florida. Miguel stood accused of kidnapping and raping an eighteen-year-old high school student. The victim alleged that Miguel had offered her a ride home from a party and then taken her to a remote location where he brutally beat and raped her. Arrested and charged with these non-bondable crimes, Miguel had been in jail for forty days before his parents came to my office.

His parents complained that the public defenders weren't doing anything for him. I had been a criminal defense attorney for over two decades, and presumed he was probably guilty. Though it happens occasionally, the police generally don't arrest innocent people.

Slowly, Miguel's parents persuaded me otherwise. They described text messages that proved Miguel wasn't even at the party where the victim was kidnapped. They wondered whether the victim had mentioned whether the perpetrator had tattoos, which was significant because Miguel's arms were covered in unique designs.

My visit with Miguel at the Miami jail fueled my belief that I might have an innocent client on my hands. He seemed so believable when he described his interaction with police after his arrest, when he passionately denied committing the abhorrent acts he stood accused of. I left the jail feeling I had to represent him. It became my mission to stick by Miguel's side until justice was served. I even reduced my fees to help Miguel and his family.

I remember how eager I was to call the prosecutor assigned to the case. I expected that as soon as I told her my client was likely innocent and provided the reasons why, she would stop the proceedings and commit to getting to the bottom of this legal mess. That's what I would have done when I was a prosecutor.

In 1992, I was hired to be a prosecutor by the head of the Miami State Attorney's Office, Janet Reno, who would later serve as U.S. Attorney General. Reno emphasized that my role as a prosecutor was to "zealously seek the truth." Because of this training, I assumed that the prosecutor in the Macias case would feel and act the same way. I expected too much from her and my high expectations made me resentful.

When I called "Tina" and shared my thoughts about Miguel's case, she listened for less than thirty seconds before she rudely cut me off. "It's almost five o'clock and I'm leaving for the day," she said dismissively. "Send me what you've got; I'll try to take a look at it this week."

I could not believe what had just happened; I had not anticipated her response and the pathetic manner in which she had spoken to me. Justice doesn't sleep. Innocent defendants need to be dealt with at all hours, even after five o'clock.

I didn't stop and think things through. Instead of responding, I reacted. "Are you kidding me?" I fired back at Tina. "You need to prioritize this *now*. I likely have an innocent client on my hands." I refused to accept "no" for an answer.

Apparently, Tina had other plans. She refused to speak with me further, especially after I became so enraged. I reacted with words I usually reserve for when I stub my toe in the middle of the night on the way to the bathroom.

Had I stopped and implemented the first step of my formula, my perspective would have been different, and the outcome would have been, too. I would have recognized and accepted that Tina approached her job differently than I had when I had been a prosecutor. I would have seen and accepted that she wasn't going to immediately dedicate her time toward uncovering the truth of this case.

In the right emotional state, I would have stopped, composed myself, and calmly said, "I'm sorry to dump this on you at the end of the day. You probably think I'm being pushy, but I think I have an innocent client who's stuck in jail. I'm sure that's not a situation either of us want. Given the late hour, can you suggest a way, perhaps through one of your colleagues, that we might take a quick look at the matter? How do you see us resolving this quickly so we can get home to our families?" My reaction, which didn't serve either the client or me well, prevented me from advancing my agenda.

Instead of easing up, I spent the next day emailing and calling Tina. My behavior—fueled by being pissed off from the day before—attempted to force Tina onto the "he might be innocent" train.

You can guess what her response was — silence. I wasted a full day while my client languished in jail. Imagine how much better those two days would have turned out had I used step one of my own happiness formula.

When I finally stopped, calmed myself, and thought things through, I was able to discover who her supervisor was and deal exclusively with her. Fortunately, her supervisor embraced the matter with the professionalism I had expected of Tina. She spoke with me at length and met with me to review the evidence. At that face-to-face meeting, the supervisor told me the victim had undergone a rape treatment examination and that the perpetrator's DNA had been sent to the lab for analysis.

While not certain of Miguel's innocence, the supervisor became concerned that law enforcement might have had an innocent defendant on their hands. She did something unexpected: She contacted the lab and requested they prioritize the analysis of the DNA evidence seized in the case. Apparently, asking them to pull this case from the bottom to the top of their to-do list was a "no-no." She asked me not to tell anyone she had done it.

I was immensely grateful, especially since I was still fuming from the treatment I had received from Tina.

Miraculously, within just a few days of her request, the prosecutor learned of the results. As expected and hoped, the DNA did not match my client. It did match someone else's. His name was Miguel Bustos, a 28-year-old who had been arrested a few years earlier for aggravated assault with a deadly weapon. His DNA was already in the system and available to prosecutors.

The supervisor immediately calendared the case for court and dropped the charges against my client. Only a few days had passed between my agreeing to represent Miguel and his charges being dropped. Miguel spent a total of 42 days in jail with no bond for a felony he hadn't committed. When I saw Tina in court, we made eye contact, but she said nothing. Expecting any sort of apology from her was setting my expectations too high.

Later on, I learned more about the backstory of the case, which shed light on why Tina had been so reluctant to entertain the possibility that my client was innocent. Tina was the one who had investigated the case after my client had been arrested. She was the one who had filed the charges. The only evidence she had

had to base her decision on was the victim's positive identification.

What troubled me even more was how the identification occured. The victim had searched on Facebook for friends of the person who had thrown the party from which she was kidnapped. She knew the name of her rapist was "Miguel" and had a mental image of what he looked like. Armed with that information, she spotted my client's face online and became convinced that he had been the offender.

In the victim's defense, Miguel Macias and Miguel Bustos share a striking resemblance. I don't harbor any ill will toward the victim, but I feel differently about Tina. Thinking about how she handled the case still gets me riled up. She cut corners and rushed to file charges. Had she followed up on leads and done her job efficiently, my client might never have been arrested.

I complicated matters — for myself and for my client — when I failed to stop and let my emotions get out of control during my call with Tina. Reacting the way I did caused me to become angry and adversely affected my client's chance of acquittal. Blinded by anger and frustration, I felt powerless to stop myself; I let my ego get in the way.

The trajectory of someone's life can be mended or mangled by how we manage our emotions. After this case, I made a vow to try not to react in the moment when faced with similar emotions.

Action Steps

1. How will step one (stopping and responding rather than reacting) be beneficial to you?

2. Take three slow, deep breaths. Describe how that makes you feel.

STEP 2: ARM (YOURSELF!)

The next step in the happiness formula is to *Arm Yourself.* To change the unwanted feelings you initially had, you stopped; that's great! The next step in my happiness formula is to *Arm Yourself.* Now stay with me ... I'm not encouraging you to run to the local pawnshop and purchase an AK-47. Mine is a peaceful solution. Instead of arming yourself with a gun, arm yourself with a *spiritual* tool belt. Picture a handyman with a tool belt strapped around his waist. In it are a hammer, screwdrivers, pliers, and a tape measure. Each tool amplifies the handyman's ability to pound, twist, grip, or measure accurately. Instead of physical tools, imagine psychological tools that hammer in the good thoughts and pry out the bad ones. You are already wearing a spiritual tool belt; you were born with one.

Even in the womb, we begin developing tools for our spiritual tool belt. Ever seen a sonogram revealing an unborn child who is sucking their thumb? That soothing tool gets used before more complex coping tools come into play.

A newborn baby adds many other tools to their spiritual tool belt. Toddlers and young children typically go to their parents when they don't feel well, physically or emotionally. They're learning the need to share emotions with others, and are subconsciously aware that doing so helps us heal. Sharing emotions with others in times of need is a spiritual tool that benefits us throughout our lives.

You could choose from an infinite number of spiritual tools to help you develop. What works for one person may not work for another. Just be aware that you *do* have a spiritual tool belt and should be prepared to use it.

Here are a few of my favorite spiritual tools. Choose the ones that work best for you:

1) Random Acts of Kindness

Random acts of kindness are small, kind, compassionate, spontaneous gestures done with minimal effort. It's simpler than handing someone the keys to a new Ferrari. Smile at a stranger, or say "good morning" when walking into a crowded elevator. The size of the gesture doesn't matter; it's the intentionality behind the gesture that matters. Other examples include paying someone a compliment, holding the door open, or paying for a stranger's meal. Practicing random acts of kindness may feel uncomfortable at first, but you can expand your happiness by embracing opportunities to show love that you would normally ignore.

A Flat Tire

One hot Saturday afternoon I was rushing from my home to meet someone at my office thirty minutes south. On my way, I got word that my client had already arrived. Crap! They had gotten there early, and I was going to be late. They were going to have to wait in the heat outside my locked office. As I drove south on I-95 (significantly above the speed limit), I noticed my dashboard lights flashing. My right front tire was losing air rapidly, forcing me to pull over. Sure enough, I discovered a significant gash in my tire, likely caused by road debris.

A Road Ranger drove up within minutes and offered to change the tire for me, free of charge. While the Ranger was working on my tire, I was surprised to see another motorist in the same situation. He, too, had suffered a flat tire. From the condition of his old, dilapidated pickup truck and the way he dressed, I figured he wasn't a man of means. The gestures he made as he gazed at his flat tire said, *How the hell am I going to deal with this? Why me?*

I decided to pass on the act of kindness I had just received. The Road Ranger had offered to replace this man's tire, too, so I needed another way to help him. I walked up to the man and handed him a $20 bill. He was confused for a moment and then, overcome with emotion, said, "God bless you." It was a small gesture, but it made me feel great. The joy that stretched across his face helped me as much as I had helped him. Embracing this opportunity to brighten someone's day left me feeling satisfied. Kindness is a gift that keeps on giving. I not only felt happy the day I helped this man; I feel happy every time I reflect on that day.

Random acts of kindness can take on a variety of forms, involving words or actions. Both are valuable. In the flat tire story, no words were necessary. I offered the $20 bill and the man received it. At other times, making eye contact with someone to acknowledge their presence in the room can make a great impact on their day. Verbally affirming your gratitude for someone also helps. Play into your strengths; any positive gesture will make a difference.

The Response to Your Kindness

The recipient's reaction to your act of kindness is irrelevant to how you allow it to make you feel. Sure, it feels nice if they express gratitude. However, for you to receive the maximum benefit of your act, you must not depend on their response. Often, you won't get the reaction you were expecting. The other person's negative response will likely have little to do with you. You may lovingly open a door for someone and have them respond by saying, "I can get my own damned door!" Remember my expectations about how the prosecutor would behave in the Miguel Macias case? *Expectations are future resentments.*

An Unexpected Response

I experienced one unexpected response to kindness immediately after entering the Miami criminal courthouse. I was in a wonderful mood that day and had arrived early to address my case first. There were very few people in the courtroom since the doors had just opened and court wasn't set to start for another ten minutes. Upon entering, I noticed two clerks of court sitting at their usual table, off to the right of where the judge sits. One seemed to be around 20 years old and was being trained by a much older clerk. The older clerk and I had been amiable toward one another during the 25-plus years I worked in the Miami criminal system.

Upon entering the courtroom, I stared at both of them and let out an enthusiastic, "Good morning, loves!" I knew what I was doing; I was sharing love with two clerks who rarely got attention unless attorneys or courtroom personnel needed something from them. I wanted to show that someone could express appreciation without following it up with requests — a random act of kindness. I hoped my energy would have a positive impact. (Selfishly, I knew I'd feel better too; I always do after performing acts of kindness.)

The younger clerk smiled back and said, "Thank you so much!" The older clerk, the one I thought was my friend, fired back, "I'd appreciate it if you didn't call me that." I had not been expecting that kind of response. I smiled because I thought she was kidding, and asked for clarification. "Are you kidding?" The intensity in her eyes and the seriousness in her face conveyed that I had offended her. I replayed what I had said when I walked into the courtroom:

"Good morning?"

No, that can't be it.

Calling her "Love?"

I fell into a several-minute monologue explaining to her how she must have received my message the wrong way. All this drama, and court hadn't even started yet!

At the conclusion of my passionate explanation, she repeated her remark. "I'd appreciate it if you didn't call me that."

I didn't get it, and I walked away feeling misunderstood.

After waiting by the podium for about fifteen seconds, eager for the judge to arrive, a voice inside me said, "Go back to her." I walked over and asked her, "Just so I can make this a learning opportunity, what part of what I said offended you?"

"You called me, 'Love.' You wouldn't call a man that, would you?"

I opened my mouth to respond, but couldn't find the right words to say. I thought about defending my position again, but the most fitting words came to me: "You're right. I wouldn't say that to a man."

After apologizing, I walked away. This unexpected interaction taught me a lot. Even when your intentions are pure, you can still treat people in a way that doesn't make them feel loved. In fact, you can make them feel the opposite. Additionally, I knew there was no need to take what she said or how she reacted personally. I committed to continue offering random acts of kindness regardless of how others might react.

The purpose of the Myers-Briggs personality test is to classify you as one of sixteen personality types. Imagine that, for every random act of kindness you perform, you could get sixteen different reactions! People and personalities are far too diverse to accurately predict what kind of reaction you will get. Rely on the person whose emotions you can always control: yourself!

2) Short Gratitude List

I fell in love with the phrase "Attitude of gratitude" when I first heard it. Not only is it a cute rhyme, I immediately connected with the message. When I'm focusing on what I am grateful for, instead of what I lack, I feel happier. Once I make this mental shift, I begin appreciating the smallest of things I used to take for granted, which opens my heart and my mind.

Every night before I go to sleep, I purposefully add something to my short gratitude list. As the list increases, my attitude of gratitude expands. I write down the date each night, and under that, I write a list of five things I experienced that day for which I'm grateful. You can add anything to the list, big or small. The only rule is that you can never repeat a list item. For example, you can only write, "I am grateful for my wife," one time. But writing "I am grateful for my wife because she cooked an amazing teriyaki chicken dish for me tonight" is different than saying, "I'm grateful for my wife who surprised me with tickets to the Springsteen concert."

The more detailed your writing, the better. As days pass and your list builds, your gratitude list will become a journal. Write anywhere — on your computer or on paper. Though I am in the habit of writing down five things, you can start with three. Studies[4] show that people who write down three things they are grateful for each day are significantly happier than those who do not. I feel like I've found a "life hack" every night when I purposely relive the best moments of my day. And I get "two-for-one"; I enjoy the moment when it occurs and then re-experience the joy of it while writing my list.

Another benefit of the short gratitude list is that you fill your head with gratitude right before you sleep. Our thoughts speed

---

4   https://www.sciencedirect.com/science/article/pii/S0022103117308569

in a thousand directions when we're lying down at night; choosing to focus on positive thoughts is a lot better than dwelling on what went wrong that day or how much you have to do the next day. The more negative your nighttime thoughts are, the greater your stress and worry, which hinders your ability to secure a great night's sleep.

3) Long Gratitude List

The long gratitude list offers the same benefits as the short gratitude list, the primary difference being that the long gratitude list isn't limited to five items. The long gratitude list has no limit at all. Keep writing, letting yourself get lost in thoughts of gratitude. List *everything* you feel grateful for. I start at the very beginning of my day and write that I'm grateful that I woke up that morning; many people won't get that privilege again. Then, I move on to the first breath I took. After that, I write that I'm grateful for the next breath and the next and the next.

I usually focus on my body for a while and express gratitude for my working limbs and inner parts that keep me alive and healthy. We often focus only on what we see without reflecting on our bodies and the miraculous processes happening inside us every hour of every day. I can spend several minutes on why I'm grateful for my kids, my wife, my family members, friends, etc. There is no end to what can be put on the long gratitude list.

While writing the long gratitude list, something magical happens: your happiness increases! There is no way to feel bad while writing a list of things you're grateful for. It's like riding on a waverunner; you never see anyone frowning while cruising across the water at 50 mph. When you center your thoughts on everything you're grateful for, you replace stinkin' thinkin' with thoughts that fill your heart with happiness.

4) Meditation

Speaking to a Higher Power — prayer — is only one component of my daily inner mission. The other component is listening to the answers I'm given — "meditation." As Supreme Master Ching Hai teaches, regardless of one's religion, those who don't take the time to listen can never be communicated with. Even when you talk to a friend who loves you dearly, you must be willing to listen. After all, there's a reason we have two ears and one mouth. Hai believes that many treat their Higher Powers worse than a friend. We keep talking all the time and give the universe no chance to be heard by us. Meditation is a time for quiet listening. I have received many answers during this cherished time.

Meditation isn't reserved for toga-wearing folks in caves or bald guys on high mountain peaks; it's for anyone willing to make time for it. At the Chopra Center in Carlsbad, California, I learned there's no such thing as a bad meditation; nor is there a right or wrong way to meditate. There are many different ways to do it, none better or worse. How you choose to meditate is a personal choice. For those who know nothing about the practice, I'll share what it means to me and how I practice it.

Whatever version of meditation you seek, the most important thing is to sit comfortably. Close your eyes and ask yourself three questions. The following three questions are part of my pre-meditation process:

"Who am I?"
"What do I want?"
"What is my purpose in life?"

Having practiced this pre-meditation process countless times, I am reminded that who I am is not made up of the roles I play as a lawyer, father, or media legal analyst. At my core, I am pure love. The same applies to you. You are not defined by your life's circumstances; we are all connected. There's an energy that binds us all. After "Who am I?" ask yourself what you truly want. I remind myself that I want serenity. If, for example, my Higher Power wants me to win the lottery or land my own national television show, that will be His decision in His time. It is not external matters that excite me, but the state of being I wish to achieve. I want peace and serenity, and I will do all I can to maintain it.

Given that you're reading this book, my guess is that you want the same.

The final step in this pre-meditation process is to ask what your life's purpose is. This might take time to discover as you learn more about yourself by listening. It took me several months to conclude that my purpose in life is to be of maximum service to both my Higher Power and my fellow man. Perhaps your life's purpose is centered around living out a dream you've suppressed for years. If you can't remember your dreams, think back to your childhood — a time in your life when you thought anything was possible. In those days, what got you excited and made you want to jump out of bed in the morning? What would make you do that again now?

After answering these questions, sit quietly for twenty minutes. That may seem like an eternity. When I first started meditating, I couldn't get past twenty seconds. My mind was filled with thoughts: *What the hell are you doing? You don't have time to meditate. There are things you should be doing. This meditation stuff is flaky and doesn't work. You're pathetic.* Practice makes perfect. None of the baseball players in the Hall of Fame hit a home run their first time at bat. I had to develop a meditation "practice." Committing to meditating twice a day, for thirty minutes per session, for ninety days helped turn my practice into a critical part of my day that I cannot forgo.

Even if only for a few minutes, take time out of your day for the most important person in your life — *yourself*. There's a reason why airlines instruct that, in the event of an emergency, you should put on your own oxygen mask first. You must take care of yourself first. If not, you will be of little value to those around you.

Start with only a minute of meditation. The next day, try five minutes. Each day, expand the time. When your mind starts to wander — and it will — focus on your breathing. Breathe in deeply and breathe out. Breathe in again and breathe out. Feel your lungs filling with air and letting it out.

Another meditation method involves focusing on a *mantra*. I use a Primordial Sound Mantra. When my mind starts wandering during meditation, I shift my thoughts to a few syllables that were given to me when I went out to the Chopra Center. These syllables — two of the three being "Om" and "Namah" — are supposed to represent the sound the Earth made when I was born.

You don't need to go to the Chopra Center or focus on a Primordial Sound Mantra to be an effective meditator. Any phrase will do — "Love and Peace," your children's names, or even "Shama lama ding dong." What *is* important is that when your thoughts wander, you learn to drift back to your mantra and allow your brain to gently focus on it.

Don't get upset about having distracting thoughts; you will have many. Even after meditating for over ten years, my thoughts pull me away from my meditation. I've learned to not punish myself for having them; they're going to happen no matter what.

All meditations are perfect. Even when the dog barks constantly, and the kids walk in on you several times, and you have constant thoughts, all meditations are perfect. In these moments when you could choose to become frustrated, tell yourself that each meditation unfolds exactly how it is supposed to.

Throughout the years, I've benefited immensely from my meditation practice. I've become a better person, in and out of court. Instead of reacting uncontrollably, I respond. My mindfulness of my surroundings has been greatly enhanced.

Regardless of its duration, I leave every meditation session feeling relaxed, peaceful, and joyful — without a care. Through meditation, I live in the *now*. All is wonderful right here, right now; nothing needs to be added or taken away. The present moment is a gift, which is why it is called the "present."

5) Change Your Mind

My wife and I love the band, Sister Hazel, and one of our favorite songs is "Change Your Mind." In that song, they ask whether you've "ever thought there might be a better way to just feel better about today." The lyrics suggest, "If you want to be somebody else, change your mind."

Making up your mind to change how you feel is the key to happiness.

Action Steps

1. Perform at least one random act of kindness. Describe how it makes you feel.

2. Write a Short Gratitude List. Commit to writing on the list every day for ninety days.

3. Write a Long Gratitude list. Describe how it makes you feel.

4. Meditate. If you've never meditated, try for just one minute. Commit to a meditation practice for the next 90 days. Increase the time you meditate each day.

STEP 3:

LOOK (FOR THE RIGHT TOOL)

Let's recap our happiness formula.

You started out feeling emotions you no longer wished to feel, so you thought of SALADS.

Remembering step one, you chose to *stop!* You breathed deeply, making sure to respond and not react.

Then you chose to *arm yourself* by putting on your spiritual tool belt, which may have included practicing random acts of kindness or a gratitude list.

The next step is to *look for the right tool*. Look down at your spiritual tool belt and select the particular tool you think will be best for changing the emotions you're feeling. Every emotion is unique; the tool you choose to change it should be unique, too. Look at the tool belt and make the strongest choice.

You won't always select the most effective tool. For example, some may choose to grab a bottle of alcohol. That's not *always* the strongest choice.

Phoning a friend to discuss what ails you may be a strong tool choice, at least until your friend starts to co-sign on your bullshit victim story. Friends mean well but sympathy can keep you stuck in your way of thinking. If their only response to your emotional heartache is that "everything's going to work itself out," they're not offering concrete advice on how to change your emotions. Instead, they're encouraging you to depend even further on factors you cannot control.

Most of my problems stemmed from fear of not having enough money. I assumed that the cure to my financial woes was to make more money. As soon as I made more money, I would be happy. I focused on increasing revenues at work — and I was successful. Do you think I was happier for it?

There's nothing wrong with making money. Stuff costs money, and with three children to provide for, I get that as much as anyone. However, there's a difference between seeking money as a resource and craving it for your happiness. As it turns out, the happier I became, the more money I made. Trial and error taught me that when I choose the pursuit of money as my spiritual tool for increasing happiness, I sell myself short and don't resolve the underlying issues.

The tool I most often choose to change my stinkin' thinkin' is being of service to others. "Service is the rent we pay for the space we take up on Earth."[5] I try paying rent as if I were taking up the entire state of Texas.

When I am of service, I am immediately transformed and brought to a happy place. Albert Schweitzer, a well-known theologian, organist, writer, humanitarian, philosopher, and physician once said, "I don't know what your destiny will be, but there's one thing I do know: Those around us who will truly be happy are those who have sought and found how to serve."

No tool works more efficiently than service to others. Service is my life's mission. Instead of representing clients to make money, I make myself of service to others and happen to get paid for my efforts. When I wake up each morning, instead of thinking about what I want from the world, I focus on what those around me need. *What can I offer others? How can I be of service to them?* This shift in perspective has been one of the keys to my happiness — and it makes a difference in the lives of those around me.

Example of Service — Violet Mendez

It was early in the day and I was swamped when I received the first call about Violet Mendez. My plate was overflowing, personally

---

5   https://www.barrypopik.com/index.php/new_york_city/entry/service_is_
the_rent_we_pay_to_live_on_this_earth

and professionally, but her father, Orlando Mendez, had been told that I was the guy to call.

His story was beyond belief: His 14-year-old daughter had been cut from her boys' middle school baseball team at Okeeheelee Middle School in West Palm Beach, Florida. The reason given for kicking her off the team was that she hadn't actually tried out. Orlando knew there must have been more behind the story, because the day before Violet was benched, a mother of one of the players told anyone who would listen that Violet was a "freak of nature," a "lesbian," "a distraction," and a "dyke." This woman thought Violet belonged on the *girls' softball* team and that she shouldn't be playing with the boys.

Violet had been on the team for two years; she was a star player. The coach told me that Violet didn't pitch very often because none of her teammates could play catcher and handle her 73-mile-per-hour fastballs. She hadn't tried out because there was no need for her to do so. At the end of the previous season, Violet had been given her uniform and told she would be on the team the following season. The "failure-to-try-out" excuse was bogus. The principal, who was new to the school, succumbed to the pressure of a cantankerous and jealous mother who didn't want her son to lose precious playing time to a girl.

Though I was swamped, I chose to be of service to Violet and her family — pro-bono. I called and emailed the principal that day, but to no avail. When she finally responded, she referred me to the school district's attorneys. Instead of doing the right thing, she chose to "lawyer up." The lawyer for the school district told me it was unfair that Violet had just walked onto the team without trying out. I relayed to her what the coach had told me, and informed her that Violet was ranked among the top 90 high school players, *even though she was still in middle school.*

Flustered, the attorney pieced together another reason why Violet couldn't be on the team — an issue that had not even come up in previous discussions. She claimed that my client hadn't turned in all the proper paperwork required to play. I explained that Violet had completed all the forms and had tried to turn them in, but that her coach had told her to hold onto them, that he would get them later. Most of the boys on the team hadn't provided paperwork to the coach either, yet none of them faced benching.

What should have been resolved with one phone call took a day. It wasn't until I crafted and sent a press release to my extensive list of local and national media contacts that I got the school's attorney to make concessions. Right before game time, with the media present and reporters covering the story, the attorney emailed me to say that if Violet's forms were in, she could play. We tendered the forms to the coach and Violet returned to the field.

A smile spread across my face that day; I had made a difference in someone's life through service.

Violet and her family were grateful for my efforts, and we remain friends to this day.

In the past, during darker times, I would have avoided their request for assistance, claiming I didn't have the time. Now I seek out opportunities like this. I will always be busy. I'll always have more paying clients and more money to make. But what makes me happy as I lay my head on my pillow each night is reflecting on the opportunities I embraced to be of service that day.

You don't have to become Mother Theresa to be happy. Whatever you select, whether it's service or another tool, give it some thought; be intentional about it. Look at the many tools available in your tool belt and be ready to use the one that will most effectively serve you (and those around you) in the moment.

Action Steps

1. Perform one act of service today. Describe how it makes you feel.

2. Commit to performing one act of service each day. List some ways you believe you can be of daily service to others.

STEP 4: ACT!

You're halfway through the happiness formula.
SALADS means:

Step 1) **Stop**
Step 2) **Arm** Yourself
Step 3) **Look** for the Right Tool

While I was writing about step four, I was reminded of something that is likely on your mind — something so predictable it's not even necessary to say: Frogs! You're thinking of frogs, right? Oh, you're not? It's just me? Either way, think of frogs when you think of step four — *act!*

Imagine three frogs on a lily pad. Two of the three frogs decide to jump off the lily pad. How many are left? The answer would seem to be one.

If one was your answer, you've just joined the ranks of the many well-intended, bright folks who have gotten this problem wrong. Let me repeat the scenario with added emphasis. Three frogs are sitting on a lily pad. Two of the frogs *decide* to jump off. How many are left? All three remain on the lily pad, because they only *decided* to jump off. Deciding to do something is not the same as actually doing it. Nothing will happen until you actually leap and move beyond deciding.

Looking for the right tool is not enough. You need to do more than say, "I *should* meditate," or "I *should* work out more." As we consume more media and are inundated with miracle solutions to our lives' problems, we accumulate more and more "shoulds." We "should" all over ourselves. Only when we replace "I should" with "I must" will we see results.

Those who create daily gratitude lists experience increased happiness, increased self-esteem, and better physical and psychological health.[6] What did I do upon learning that? Absolutely nothing. Sure, I thought about it for a while. I said to myself, *I should* start writing gratitude lists. I even started to think of things for which I was grateful. That helped a little but I still didn't take action and write those things down.

I went as far as lecturing others, preaching that they needed to keep a gratitude list. I told them of the benefits, even when I had not taken action myself.

---

6   https://greatergood.berkeley.edu/pdfs/GratitudePDFs/2Wood-Grati-tudeWell-BeingReview.pdf

I finally shifted my thinking: *I* (must) *keep a daily list where I'll write down the top five things for which I'm most grateful.* As soon as I convinced myself of the vital need, I began writing the list and saw immediate change.

Similarly, when I told myself and others that, "I must meditate every day," I gave up any "wiggle room." I made a commitment and took action. Once I took action, I experienced the change I desperately needed.

Taking Action with a Friend

We had the case in the bag. Given my experience as a prosecutor, a colleague asked for my help. He was prosecuting a violent, career criminal accused of armed robbery. What my colleague lacked in trial skills, he made up for in kindness. He was the nicest guy around, and a good friend.

The evidence we presented was considerable and compelling. We had just called our last witness, a cop, though I didn't think we should have called him to testify. He had only shown up at the crime scene to haul the defendant off to jail; he had played no pertinent role in the investigation. By all accounts, we had won. Our evidence was strong and we should have rested our case. But this was my partner's case; I was helping out, happy to get the trial experience.

The officer took the stand, and my colleague asked him a few questions about his role transporting the accused to jail. As expected, his answers added nothing noteworthy to our case.

When my partner finished his line of questioning, he asked the judge if he could have a moment to confer with me.

When he came over to the prosecution table, I whispered, "That's all. You covered it. Let the defense have him, and let's rest."

My colleague turned back to the judge, but he didn't say, "Nothing further, your Honor." His face lit up as if he'd had some kind of epiphany. "Just one more question, your Honor," he said.

I saw everything in slow motion. *Oh, no. This cannot be good.*

In his most confident voice, my colleague asked his witness, "Officer, do you see the person you transported in the courtroom today?"

Oh, shit! I saw O.J. Simpson struggling to pull on the little glove and Johnnie Cochran making his famous pronouncement: "If it doesn't fit, you must acquit."

"I do," answered Officer Friendly, pointing to the defense table. "That's him right there." Three people sat at the defense table; it wasn't clear to whom he was pointing.

"Can you describe what that person is wearing?" the judge asked.

"Yes, your Honor," the witness said. "He's the one wearing the blue, pin-striped suit with the red tie."

The three people sitting at the defense table included two black men and one white man. The white man and one of the two black men wore suits. The other black guy wore a button-down shirt and khakis — no tie. The defendant was the one *not* wearing a tie! To the courtroom's shock, the defendant's black attorney had just been identified as the perpetrator who had been taken to jail!

I give credit to the defense attorney for not laughing out loud. He developed his closing argument around the cop's flawed identification. He confidently told the jury, "Ladies and gentlemen, I couldn't have scripted this any better myself." When it came time for the jury's final decision, a bad guy who should have been locked in prison for decades walked away.

That my colleague's witty decision led to such an unfavorable outcome pissed me off. I let my partner have it. His "one question too many" cost us the trial. Venting my anger and frustration, I made him imagine all the victims who would suffer thanks to this guy being free instead of behind bars where he belonged. What infuriated me even more was my trial partner's reaction: he didn't get it. He became defensive and failed to accept responsibility for his actions.

This poured fuel on the fire. I made a number of personal jabs at him, making remarks that were offensive and over the line. My words hurt him greatly, but I didn't feel bad.

As the days passed, I felt increasingly uncomfortable about the way I had spoken to my colleague. After I had had time to cool down, I realized he had been doing the best he could, given his level of awareness and experience. He didn't mean to lose the trial. I had taken the trial loss personally — and it was about to cost me his friendship.

Knowing I had engaged in behavior that didn't serve me well didn't sit right with me. I needed to speak with him. But I didn't do anything! I *thought* about doing something; I *thought* about it quite often. *I should go speak to him. I should apologize.*

Although I saw the steps I needed to take to make the situation right, I failed to act.

Once I changed my thoughts from "I *should*" to "I *must*," I stepped into action. I arranged the meeting I had spent way too much time thinking about, and said what I had been longing to say to him. He graciously accepted my apology, and even apologized for the role he had played.

To this day, we remain friends. Taking action was the key to seeing this problem solved and enjoying increased happiness.

Action Steps

1. List three tasks you know you should do, that you are willing to change to I must do.

2. For the next 90 days, commit to accomplishing those must-do tasks.

STEP 5: DECIDE!

If you've decided to take action, you're ready for step five. Step five requires you to *decide!* How will you *choose* to feel? If you feel better after using your spiritual tools, what follows is the decision to *remain* feeling better, and not slide back into stinkin' thinkin'.

Training your thinking is like training for a marathon. When you first start training, the most you walk in a day is from your couch to the fridge. You make a plan to change your habits by eating cleaner and getting outside more. You take baby steps, running longer distances each week. Finally, the much-awaited race day arrives. You are healthy, and you finish the race in less time than you expected. You feel great and proud of yourself! While talking with friends at the finish line, you agree to run the same marathon next year.

On Monday after race day, you're tired. You decide to sink back into your comfy couch. You're already in good shape, so you believe that training for the next race won't be necessary. You'll be able to run the second marathon without the hard work you put in for the first one.

Is it possible to succeed in next year's marathon without any training? You'll be out of breath by mile two … and will quit by mile five.

Seeing real change in our thoughts and emotions requires intentional decisions. If we lose our intentionality one day, we slip back into our old selves. Keep training your thoughts and emotions to keep seeing results.

The most important concept to take away from step five is that *happiness is a decision.* Aristotle said, "Take charge of your thoughts; you can do what you will with them." Happiness is a decision. Happiness is your choice. Whatever you will is what will happen. Your happiness is up to you and it's not contingent upon external elements.

Easier said than done, Mark. I can't just decide *to be happy. How I feel depends on what happens to me at any given moment.*

I used to think that too, but I didn't like how that made me feel. The reason I went into the happiness field is that I was tired of having my emotions dictated by external factors, like how the people around me behaved. I wanted tools that would assist me with being happier, regardless of my circumstances.

Imagine your boss walked up to you one day and said, "Our company is launching a new employee benefit plan, and you have two options: You can either accept a pay rate that changes every day, based on how your co-workers perform. Or, you can have your pay based on how *you* perform." Imagine how stressful it would be to let your financial future be determined by other people's performance? We do this every day with our thoughts and emotions.

When introducing the happiness formula, I shared the words, "Thought, feeling, action." First we have a *thought*. Then that thought makes us *feel* a certain way. How we feel dictates how we *act*. The key to Step 5 and to feeling happier is to focus on your thoughts.

To accomplish this, we must analyze the *source* of our thoughts. Take a look at the organ in your head — you know, the one the scarecrow searched for in the *Wizard of Oz*. I'm talking about your brain! It's the most complex machine on the planet, made up of over 100 trillion connections and 100 billion neurons.

When the Brain Serves You Well

The brain serves you well in a myriad of ways: It controls your muscles. Good luck running from a ferocious dog without your brain informing your legs to kick into high gear. Try lifting your groceries without your brain telling your muscles to move. What organ tells your eyes to focus on the next words in this book? Every physical action we take involves our muscles, which are controlled by the brain.

The brain controls your organs. While reading this book, have you had to tell your heart to pump blood? Have you had to tell your lungs to breathe? These bodily functions happen because the brain continually tells our organs what to do, twenty-four hours a day, every day of our lives. When writing your gratitude list, consider expressing gratitude for your brain, an under-appreciated organ that assisted in securing the last breath you took, and the one you'll take after that, and the one after that....

When the Brain Does *Not* Serve You Well

Your brain doesn't always serve you well. Sometimes an endless line of incessant chatter fills your head, each thought racing a different way, each vying for your attention.

I used to think there was something wrong with me. Maybe I had a problem because I was always thinking, every day and every night. Like a water faucet that drips constantly, my brain was always going. Thought after thought ran rapid-fire between my ears. It never seemed to stop. Did I have ADD? ADHD?

I came to learn that I wasn't alone; there was nothing wrong with me. The average person has between 12,000 to 60,000 thoughts per day.[7] No longer did I feel odd for having endless thoughts bouncing around my head each day.

And I wasn't the only one surrounded by thoughts that didn't serve me well. I was bombarded by "negative thoughts," every day.

---

7   2005, National Science Foundation

It's no wonder I struggled to be happy. My active brain ensured that couldn't happen.

Your brain is like your colon; they both produce crap! About 80% of those 12,000–60,000 thoughts we have each day don't serve us well. And approximately 95% of the thoughts we will have today are the same thoughts we had yesterday. We are stuck in a vicious cycle. *Get me off this crazy psychological treadmill!*

Sit quietly for a moment. Notice all those thoughts that don't serve you well. Have you ever sat in a noisy restaurant for an hour before finally tuning in to hear the music that's been playing in the background the entire time? Slow down to focus on these negative thoughts, and you'll realize they are all fear-based. Fear is an acronym for "False Evidence Appearing Real." We always imagine the worst possible scenario, but 99% of the time, the worst-case situation never occurs. We are programmed to be cautious.

Cavemen had to think constantly of worst-case scenarios; survival depended on it. It would have been foolish to walk willy-nilly into a dark cave without considering that a ferocious animal might be waiting inside. External threats required cavemen to think things through and prepare for every adverse scenario.

The thought process that served cavemen well continues to protect us today, yet it also impinges on our happiness. Being cautious by looking both ways before crossing the street is prudent. Practicing a healthy concern for one's safety is necessary for survival, even in the bubble-wrapped world we live in. Yet, too many of us take it to an extreme. Instead of a healthy dose of concern, we choose to embrace overwhelming thoughts of fear that leave us emotionally paralyzed and unhappy.

The brain interferes with our well-being by consistently and systematically sending us fear-based thoughts — fears of things like public speaking, heights, bugs, flying, enclosed spaces, needles, public spaces, drowning, strangers, and darkness, among others.

In addition to sending us common phobias, our brains make us criticize ourselves and compare ourselves to our peers. *Just look at her; look at how pretty she is. You're not nearly as pretty.* Or, *Look at him; he's so successful. You're nothing compared to him.* Our thoughts get out of hand: *You're fat. Just look at you. No matter what you do, you will always be fat. Not only are you fat, you're stupid, too. You'll never amount to anything.* Our brains never give us a break.

Our brains discipline us. *You are a bad person; you should be punished.* It's as if my brain occupied all the seats of the Supreme Court, always has the majority, and always gets its way — a never-ending cycle.

We begin to believe at a young age that we need to listen to all of our thoughts. Our brains tell us, "Don't touch the hot stove." or, "You have a horrible voice and should never sing in public again." The thoughts keep pouring in. We erroneously believe that our thoughts define who we are.

We take our thoughts too seriously, and we embrace thoughts that don't serve us well.

But you can ignore your thoughts. In fact, you should ignore *all* the thoughts that don't serve you well. Look at each thought as merely an idea for consideration.

It's a buffet table. The chef prepares everything, but you get to take what you like and leave the rest; you don't have to put everything on your plate. Gather and embrace those thoughts that serve you well, and leave the rest. Ask your brain to send you more helpful thoughts, and relish in the joy they bring you. And when your brain sends you stinkin' thinkin', tell it you won't be entertaining or embracing those thoughts. Let them go.

Name Your Brain

The idea of giving your brain a name may seem weird. I get that. So don't do it. In fact, why not just stop reading the book and throw it in the garbage?

I don't really mean that; I'm simply acting like your brain does. That organ, which has been guiding you for your entire life, is determined to get in the way of your happiness. When your brain hears you're going to assign it a name, it doesn't like that. Your brain, the most complex machine on the planet, already knows why I'm asking you to give it a name. Your brain knows I'm trying to help you change your relationship with it.

By giving your brain a name, you anchor your belief that your brain is separate from who you are. The specific, unique name you select for your brain may remind you of the role your brain plays.

I call my brain "Biff" after the character in the *Back to the Future* movies. In the same way Biff bullied Michael J. Fox's famous character, Marty McFly, your brain has been bullying you since you were very young. Your challenge is to stand up to your inner bully. I do every day, and I love the results. When Biff sends me thoughts that don't serve me well, I smile and say, "Biff, I know what you're doing. Now knock it off. I'll be ignoring all the thoughts you send me that don't support me. If you decide to start sending me thoughts that actually serve me well, I'll start paying attention to you."

When your brain sends you thoughts that don't serve you well, be gentle with it. Don't get upset when you receive thoughts you don't want. These thoughts have been filling your head since you were young; you can't expect them to just stop. What you can change, starting now, is how you react when these thoughts appear. You have three options for dealing with any thought your brain sends to you:

- Let it go
- Embrace it
- Change it

We've already discussed options one and two, which are letting go of and embracing the thoughts your brain sends you. The third option involves *changing* your thoughts. Do this when you receive thoughts you want to let go of but can't. Such thoughts linger, always coming back around no matter what you do.

Coping with Loss

I thought I was ready for my mom's passing. She had been sick with colon cancer for eighteen months, and I had watched that insidious disease slowly ravage her body. I treated this process the way I treat other important matters in my life. I pretended my mom's life was already over. Filled with regrets, I imagined I could go back and treat my mom better without making poor decisions and incurring guilt.

I gave myself a second chance. I told my mom everything I needed to say, and I did everything I thought I needed to. I made sure she was as comfortable as possible, and ensured her final days were the best they could possibly be. I made sure my loved ones did the same. I was proud of how I handled myself in a tragic situation. At her funeral, while others mourned her death, I celebrated her life. *I had this grieving thing down.*

A few days after her passing, I was driving to the courthouse. About the only thing I enjoyed about that lengthy drive was the morning conversations with my mother. Out of habit, I reached for my phone, and in that moment, it sunk in. *I can't speak with my mother anymore. I will never get to hear her enthusiastic, loving, New York accent again.* There was nothing I could do; an immense sadness fell over me.

Seeing that I was down, Biff flooded me with negative thoughts to make me suffer even more. "Hey Mark, not only won't you ever be able to call her again, she won't be at your daughter's play premiere. She sure would have loved to have seen her precious granddaughter perform as the lead in *The Diary of Anne Frank*."

Biff wasn't even close to being done. "Oh yeah, and she won't be there for Owen's (my youngest son) Bar Mitzvah." As if that wasn't enough, Biff finished with, "Come to think of it Mark, you know she won't be at anything anymore — no more holiday events — Thanksgiving, birthdays, graduations, you name it; she won't be attending. How does that make you feel, Mark?"

Shitty, I thought.

I embraced the formula: *Do I want to feel shitty?*

"No," I told myself.

I chose to *stop* (step one).

I *arm myself* (step two) with my spiritual tool belt

I *looked for the right spiritual tool* (step 3)

And I chose to *act* (step 4).

Then I was able to *decide* (step 5) whether I wanted to remain unhappy or not.

I selected a tool I use often. I chose to change my mind about the sad realities Biff was throwing in my face. I chose to shift my perspective to love and gratitude. *Wait a minute. Sure, my mom is no longer with me, but I was fortunate to have her in my life for fifty wonderful years. Many people wish they could have had that much time with their mothers. Also, while she's not physically with me anymore, I feel her presence; she will always be with me. She can see my daughter's play — and she won't even have to buy a ticket! She will be smiling and enjoying her granddaughter's exceptional performance. With this new philosophy, I acted differently. Instead of acting sad whenever her name was mentioned, I smiled. My wife and kids appreciated my new response to something that had once brought me discomfort and pain.*

While I couldn't change the unfortunate circumstance of my mother's passing, I *was* able to change my reaction to it. A simple shift in perspective changed the way I thought, which changed the way I felt.

More Shifts in Perspective

Knowing that you possess the tools to manifest joy at any time is like having a superpower. No longer are you a slave to external forces. You can shift your perspective and immediately change from sadness or fear, to joy and freedom.

Even things I've always loved to do have, at times, become stale and mundane. I've loved going to court for over 25 years. I love the stories, the challenges, the drama, the heartache, the lessons, everything. But as strong as my enthusiasm is about court, the experience began to grow old. Even chocolate cake can get a bit ho-hum if you get too much of it. That's what going to court started to feel like.

Because my work as a trial lawyer would require me to attend court for the next several decades, I had to change my perspective. My thoughts about court needed to change, *fast*. As I had done with my mother's death, I began to focus on gratitude. By focusing on how fortunate I was to be going to court in the first place, I was able to change my perspective. I reminded myself that I am in an elite group of folks who get paid to do what they love while fighting for the liberties of their clients. Thoughts like, *This is getting a little repetitive and stale* didn't serve me, so I shifted my perspective to gratitude and joy.

Immediately after this shift I opened myself up again to experiencing the magic and miracles that occur in court. As I was exiting a courtroom, I smiled at a police officer, who was entering. He smiled back at me with a grin that conveyed, *Hey brother, thanks for smiling at me. I appreciate your act of kindness.* I glanced down at the name sewed into his uniform, and I was blown away by what I saw: "L. Innocent." *Officer Innocent?* I may be making much ado about nothing, but the encounter made me smile. Discovering the existence of "Officer Innocent" was one of many returns I received after I chose to come to court with a positive mindset.

Gummy Bear Story

One of my cases made shifting my perspective difficult. Every day leading up to a difficult trial brought more frustration and torment.

My client had been charged with possession of "candy." By "candy," I mean gummy bears, and by gummy bears, I mean those infused with THC (marijuana). When I say "possession of," I mean "trafficking." This client had attempted to move serious amounts of this unlawful product. Boxes were piled up to his car's ceiling.

After stopping him for speeding in Fort Myers, Florida, the cops sensed he was up to no good. Perhaps they were tipped off, or maybe it was just luck. The officers expended little effort to persuade my client to permit a full search of his vehicle. They hit the motherlode that day. The man was arrested and charged with drug trafficking. After bonding out, he learned he was facing prison time — up to thirty years with a three-year minimum. For quite some time, he had lawfully transported these types of gummies throughout California, where marijuana is legal. He was in Florida for a poker tournament. His mistake was bringing boxes of illegal product through the Sunshine State.

After hiring me to defend him, I contacted the prosecutor. I explained to her that my client, approaching thirty years old, had never been arrested before. I filled her ear with other persuasive, mitigating facts. I was convinced she would hand over probation on a silver platter.

Unfortunately, my expectations were far from reality. She lectured me on how things were more conservative in her jurisdiction on the West coast of Florida than they were in "liberal" South Florida, where I practice. She warned me I'd be in for a rude awakening. She blindly assumed that her office wouldn't allow her to waive the three-year minimum mandatory prison term.

I was stunned, but instead of letting my emotions get the best of me, I chose to stay calm and use my spiritual tools. *You've been at this juncture countless times in your career. What seems like an insurmountable challenge will eventually yield the just outcome you seek.*

As the case progressed, the prosecutor never changed her tune. Her office would not authorize anything but a prison sentence for my client. That left two possible options: One was going to trial. I immediately rejected this option because the only chance we had of winning this case would be to hire David Copperfield to make all those THC-filled gummies disappear. Since that wasn't a viable or affordable option, we were left with only one way to try for a favorable outcome: We would have to plead guilty before the judge and then present mitigating evidence to show why my client deserved leniency. As a lawyer, putting your client's future in the hands of a single judge is a scary proposition; we had no idea what position the judge would take.

Before choosing to have my client sentenced, I still had to take the depositions (sworn statements) of the five officers listed as state witnesses in the case. I didn't think it would help. I never envisioned any of them testifying, "Well, we pulled him over for no reason, and then performed an unlawful search of his vehicle." I pictured five "Joe Friday" types showing up with venom for my client, spewing to the court stenographer how the gummies were lawfully obtained by the police, and why there was no basis whatsoever to disregard the seized contraband as evidence.

I dreaded the day I would have to take the police officers' statements; I knew nothing favorable would come from it; it would all be a waste of time. Even worse, I would have to spend two hours driving across Florida to get to Fort Myers and another two hours coming back.

The morning finally arrived. *Crap! I'll be trapped in my car for most of the day. This sucks! And when I arrive, I'll be questioning officers who won't show the slightest interest in helping my case. What a total waste of time!* Wrapped in these thoughts, I chose to speak to Biff. I didn't speak to him out loud (because speaking to your brain out loud is definitely odd). *Hey Biff, listen ... I don't like the thoughts you're sending my way. Come on dude, I'm a professional speaker. I get paid to deliver keynote addresses to audiences, guaranteeing they can change their minds about anything and become happy. Send me some thoughts that serve me well.*

It didn't take long for me to receive the first thought that benefited me. My first shift in perspective was to no longer see myself as trapped in the car all day. I chose to acknowledge that I had the *opportunity* to spend considerable time in my "mobile office." That was a good thing, because I could use my phone and connect with whomever I wanted. I would enjoy several hours of uninterrupted space to think, and even meditate — with my eyes open, of course. I could listen to satellite radio with a few hundred stations at my fingertips if I pleased. What was dreadful became enjoyable and beneficial.

The next challenge was the deposition. I knew I would have to change my perspective if I was going to turn that into an enjoyable experience. Biff offered some thoughts that helped. *Instead of pouting your way through a deposition, why not turn it into an experiment?* I used the two-hour car ride to plan the details. No portion of it would be left to chance. The plan developed as I spoke with several friends. I was so entrenched in the various discussions that I forgot I was even in my vehicle. Driving turned out to be no hassle at all.

I implemented my plan as soon as I arrived in Fort Myers. I pulled into a gas station, the first one I saw as I exited the long interstate. I parked, walked into the store, and made a beeline for the candy section, and picked up two decent-sized bags for $1.50. These bags of candy were obviously old and ignored, given the thick layer of dust that covered them.

What kind of candy did I buy? My plan was to shower each officer with kindness. As each one would come into the room for their scheduled deposition, I would offer him a tasty treat. The candy I selected to serve was none other than gummy bears! I could think of no more appropriate treat. (Delicious as they may be, donuts wouldn't have made as much sense under these circumstances.)

The next task required for my experiment was to locate the perfect container in which to serve the gummies. I needed to make their decision of whether to eat them or not more challenging.

I served the gummies in a small, white, unmarked Styrofoam container, like the ones used by restaurants for take-out side salads. The officers would have no idea where the gummies came from and, more importantly, what added ingredients they might contain. I had a blast speaking with a number of my friends during the drive, all of whom were thoroughly vested in the outcome of this amusing experiment. I also shared what I was doing with numerous employees at the court reporter's office where the deposition-turned-experiment was to take place.

I wondered whether the officers might feel as if I was mocking their arrest. I imagined them believing they had snagged the "Tony Montana" of the gummy bear world. By Miami's standards, my client was a mere guppy. To the cops and prosecutors on the West Coast, he was a big fish.

The first cop walked into the room, and the experiment began! He sat at the long conference table. To his right sat the serious, young female prosecutor. I sat across the table from the officer. The stenographer asked him to raise his right hand and provided him with the oath. He swore to tell the truth.

"Officer, before we begin, I'd like to offer you a treat." I gently pushed the salad container filled with colorful gummies towards him. He didn't wait more than a second before plunging his right hand — the one that had just been in the air for the oath — straight into the salad container. He repeated that action several times, each time gripping several gummies and popping them into his mouth. I was shocked.

The stenographer asked him, "Don't you get the irony?"

He looked at her, dumbfounded.

She continued, "You know, gummy bears … and what the defendant was charged with?"

He shrugged his shoulders as if to say, "Don't matter to me" or, "I'm not sure what 'irony' means."

I smiled from ear to ear. I couldn't believe *any* officer would eat those gummies in the way they were served, especially given the charges of the case. Surely, this was a fluke. I figured he was the only cop who would dare partake. I couldn't wait until the second cop walked in.

Cop #2, a slightly older officer, strolled into the room. Just like cop #1, he faced the stenographer, raised his right hand, and swore to tell the truth, the whole truth, and nothing but the truth. Before he could begin his testimony, I slid the to-go container in his direction and offered him the treats. He plunged his hand right in.

As he chomped down on the gummies, the stenographer asked him, "You do understand there is marijuana in those, don't you?"

The cop's face lit up with a healthy smile. "The more the merrier!" He threw more gummies down his gullet.

The experiment had already far exceeded anything I could have expected. I was stunned, amazed, and thoroughly entertained.

How did the remaining three cops react to my unconventional undertaking? Officer #3, whose physique mirrored that of Arnold Schwarzenegger in his prime, pleasantly responded, "No thank you," and explained that he doesn't eat any sugar. That didn't come as a surprise to me, judging by his chiseled arms.

Officer #4 also declined. For some reason, I failed to ask him why, but I wish I had.

I was most concerned with officer #5's reaction. He was the lead officer, the one I felt would be the most cantankerous. If anyone was going to perceive that I was mocking the officers' efforts with my experiment, it was going to be him.

In he walked with a warm smile on his face. He looked nothing like the crusty old, humorless cop I had anticipated. He appeared a lot younger than I had envisioned and seemed like a guy I would have gotten along with in college. Despite my initial worries, he accepted my offer to eat the candy. He actually ate more gummies than the two other cops combined.

He turned out to be the coolest of the five. We took photos together, featuring what remained in the Styrofoam to-go box, and then bonded for a while after the deposition had concluded.

By devising and executing this experiment, I had succeeded in changing my perspective on the day. I had a wonderful time planning, implementing, and then reminiscing about the experience. I still become happy every time I share this story. That day, I proved to myself that what I had been preaching in my seminars actually works. While you can't change the people and circumstances around you, you can *always* change how you feel and react to them.

What ultimately happened to my gummy-bear-trafficking client? I hadn't devised the experiment for any reason other than to entertain myself and change the way I felt that day. I didn't have any intentions of using it to manipulate others or positively impact the case, though I'll admit I'm not above that if it will possibly result in a better outcome for my client. I take my pledge to implement any and all legal maneuvers to obtain the best possible outcome seriously.

This gummy case was different. I figured this prosecutor wouldn't be able to help me in any way. The prosecutor would never change her position. I was going to have my client plead guilty before the judge, and then wait to hear the sentence. Therefore, I figured I had nothing to lose and nothing to gain by conducting the experiment, even if it meant pissing off the cops or the prosecutor.

At sentencing, the prosecutor predictably requested that the judge sentence my client to a lengthy-term of incarceration. This didn't surprise me; but what *did* surprise me was the *manner* in which she requested the penalty. She didn't aggressively demand prison time. She just *asked,* as if to say, "Hey judge, I've got to take this position on behalf of my office. However, it's ultimately in your hands." She failed to highlight numerous facts that could have made my client's actions seem more egregious. For example, police had seized my client's cellphone, so the prosecutor knew from his text messages that this wasn't an isolated incident; he had made other large trafficking deals. She also didn't stress the *volume* of gummies he was caught with. While she did mention it, she didn't emphasize it as much as I had expected.

I believe the reason the prosecutor took this mild approach at sentencing was in large part because of how we had bonded over the gummy bears. She knew she had to do her job, yet she didn't want to hurt my position in the process. Her more liberal stance resulted, in my opinion, from what had taken place in the experiment.

The judge's final decision for my client's sentence? He announced that my client would only receive a few years of probation! The judge also granted our request to "withhold adjudication," which meant that he wasn't branded a convicted felon and could move to seal his record once the probation was terminated. I never expected such a favorable outcome.

Miracles occur when you zealously and strategically prioritize your spiritual health.

"Business of Is-Ness"

Another shift in perspective that has a profound impact on psychological health relates to reducing judgment. "Judgment is the thief of serenity." Do all you can to stop judging people, places, and events. Resist the temptation to label things as "good or bad, right or wrong." Instead, challenge yourself to say, "It just *is*." Make your goal to be in the "business of is-ness." Judging is a tough habit to quit; we've been judging for most of our lives. Every time we watch television, listen to the radio, or read, we are bombarded with judgment. I, along with several of my family members, have won Olympic medals in judgment (and in guilt too), but judgment doesn't serve us well. In fact, it interferes with one of my primary goals in life — being happy.

When things happen to us, we label them as "good or bad," or "right or wrong." When we hear that someone is getting a divorce, we might say, "Oh, how unfortunate. That's too bad." Is it actually bad? A divorce can serve both partners well if the relationship has become toxic or run its course.

"What about running late for work? That has to be bad, right? Well, not if you meet your future spouse on the next train."

For years, I stressed out when traffic prevented me from getting to the courthouse on time. I pictured an angry judge waiting for me to walk in who would yell at me for holding up their courtroom. As it turns out, this has rarely happened during my lengthy career. All too often, judges aren't even on the bench when I arrive. Or, if they are, they are busy handling other cases on their crowded dockets. I have changed my mindset about running late. I no longer label it as "bad." It just *is*. Invariably, it all works out in the end, and I get to avoid adding unneeded stress to my life.

I read of a woman from England whose train was delayed for four hours. Instead of getting angry, she chose to be productive. She used the time to develop ideas for a book she had wanted to write. During the delay, she found a napkin and jotted down some ideas about a boy who would fly around on a broomstick and study wizardry. This woman, J.K. Rowling, turned her "bad" situation into the creation of the international blockbuster, *Harry Potter,* which made her one of the richest people in the world. Missing a train or a flight can easily be perceived as a "bad" thing, until you meet the person of your dreams on the next train or flight. Or perhaps you'll encounter a celebrity you've been dying to meet, or someone who gives you the job of a lifetime.

Surely something as extraordinary as winning millions would be an exception to the "is-ness" rule? No; it still just *is*. I'm not saying I wouldn't want to come into millions of dollars. I could donate a fortune to a charity and ensure the financial security of my family. But look at the studies concerning most lottery winners. Most experience a significant spike in happiness immediately following the news of their winning. And then they suffer a significant *decline* in happiness, leading to bankruptcy and even suicide. I was shocked to hear of lottery winners who regretted ever having bought a ticket in the first place.[8]

Avoid labeling things as good or bad, or right or wrong. Avoid the emotional connotations that come with labels. If you choose to deem something as "bad," you subconsciously choose to create the pain that goes with a bad situation.

An Unlikely Co-Star

Resisting labeling things as "good or bad, right or wrong" is a daily challenge. It's difficult to make a dramatic shift in your mindset after decades of practicing one way of thinking.

I had been bubbling with excitement for months. In a couple of weeks, I would head to Los Angeles to shoot a television pilot for a major network.

The show starred me and two other high-profile attorneys who, in each episode, would examine a well-known trial and yield an opinion as to whether the defendant deserved a retrial. Months of planning had gone into my decision to participate in the pilot.

---

8   The study, led by researchers out the Stockholm School of Economics, Stockholm University and New York University, was circulated by the National Bureau of Economic Research as a working paper in 2019. Also: In 1978, a trio of researchers at Northwestern University and the University of Massachusetts attempted to answer this by asking two very disparate groups about the happiness in their lives: recent winners of the Illinois State Lottery — whose prizes ranged from $50,000 to $1 million — and recent victims of catastrophic accidents, who were now paraplegic or quadriplegic.

I had worked diligently with several producers to ensure the show would be done in the most efficient and accurate way possible. I had created a meaningful bond with my two other castmates.

I was filled with positive energy until, out of nowhere, I received a call from the producer. "We're considering adding a fourth attorney to co-star with you. We're reaching out to see what you think."

My initial reaction was, "No!" without even knowing who it was. For many reasons, I considered the addition of a fourth lawyer at the eleventh hour to be a "bad" thing.

The producer continued, "We're asking you, Mark, because she is a very 'controversial' figure."

I was intrigued yet concerned. Then she said it — the only name out of the *seven billion* people on this Earth I would have put on my list of people to never, *ever* work with. I felt like I had been struck in the gut. "Nancy Grace," the producer said. Only that name could have stirred up such a negative response within me.

Nancy Grace is a well-known, controversial television journalist, legal commentator, and former Georgia prosecutor. Her show, *Nancy Grace,* which ran from 2005 to 2016 on *Headline News* ("HLN", CNN's sister station), featured her signature outspoken style, as she fought for victims' rights.

I felt she routinely *trampled* on the rights of the accused.

My disdain for Nancy Grace went back years. I had judged her as someone who didn't really believe in the presumption of innocence, and who treated her guests in an unfair and rude manner. I had appeared on her show several times, and vowed I'd never return, regardless of the massive exposure I had received. One of her many shortfalls, I believed, was that she would always cut you off while you were speaking. The message you conveyed to viewers hinged upon where in the sentence you were when she rudely interrupted you. I questioned her sincerity and didn't want to be of service on her show.

When the producers told me of her potential involvement, I didn't vocalize how I felt. I figured (correctly), that they had already hired her and were informing me, rather than securing my opinion.

I found it *incredibly* challenging to go from, "This is really bad," to "Hey, this just *is*." I'm not sure I had fully arrived at "is-ness" when she walked up to me on the first day of shooting. I recall her being surrounded by people, including the executive producer of the show. Her first words (in that irritating Southern accent) were, "I hear you don't like me."

Bewildered, I slowly responded, "Um, well, I wouldn't say I don't like you; I don't know you." I paused for a moment and felt compelled to add more, since I needed to remain true to myself.

Had I not continued, I would have left her and her posse with the impression that I was okay with her. "What I don't like is how you treat people. When I was on your show, you would always cut me off. I could never get across what I wanted."

I had her attention so I continued, "It's like that song from the 90s group, Lit. The chorus goes: 'You make me com-, you make me complete, you make me completely miserable.'"

Nancy and her companions smiled.

"You see, Nancy, where you cut someone off can change the entire meaning of what they are attempting to convey."

She responded passionately, "Mark, it's shtick!"[9] I was taken aback. I hadn't picked up that her on-air behavior was all a big act for ratings. In that moment, I chose to believe, "Okay Mark, working with her just *is*. It's not bad anymore; it just *is*." I repeated that a few times to myself, and so it became.

My experience working with Nancy could not have been any better. She was professional, kind, courteous, and compassionate. Throughout the days of shooting, I got to know her and realized that most of what she did on-air was just "shtick," as she had alleged. Since that time in L.A., I have worked with her on other projects and today I consider her a friend. Never in a million years would I have bet on that occurring.

---

9   A gimmick, comic routine, or style of performance associated with a particular person.

I wasted every precious second I spent fearing having to work with her. If I had had some faith and simply thought, *It just is,* even when I couldn't see the outcome, I would have been better served.

Challenge yourself to stay in the *business of is-ness* even in scenarios that appear horrible.

The Less You Judge, the More You Can Help

The story the sixteen-year-old victim told the cops was that she had been dating my client for several months before calling off the relationship. A few days later, she claimed, my client and one of his friends showed up at her house when her mother was away. When she refused to let them in, my client supposedly asked if she would loan him her cellphone to make a call. When she opened the door to pass him the phone, the two allegedly pushed their way into the house, and according to her, proceeded to rape her. My client and his buddy were now sitting in jail, charged not only with sexual battery, but also with breaking and entering. They potentially faced life sentences.

I almost never take this kind of case. As much as I pride myself on ridding myself of judgment, I haven't always been that way. Before I learned that "judgment is the thief of serenity," I judged everything. As quickly as a cowboy could pull out his gun and fire his six-shooter, I could size things up and fling a label on them — good or bad, right or wrong, or any number of variations.

I stuck a "guilty" label on this client before I even knew the facts. Though I had been a criminal defense attorney for quite some time, I was never so gullible as to always believe in my clients' innocence. I felt a strong hesitation to take the case, given the horrific acts of which the defendants were accused.

One day, something changed. I realized that details might have been omitted from the case. I don't know what led me to have those thoughts — they just came — but I changed my way of thinking. Instead of labeling my client as "guilty" or "wrong" or "bad," I chose to believe, "it just *is*." *Who am I to judge him?* I decided to take the case and let the process run its course. I knew I'd at least have a front-row seat to wsomething entertaining.

I didn't know whether to believe my client or not. He claimed the sex was consensual. He *seemed* believable, however, I had my doubts about whether his claim was accurate. The prosecutor believed the victim's side of the story; he offered thirty years as a plea bargain against the possibility of a life sentence if the case went to trial.

During my investigation of the case, we discovered an interesting document. Written in the victim's own handwriting were two pages entitled, "Incidents." Each page contained several men's names, along with cryptic numbers, words, symbols, and dates. The first name listed was "Marlon." Under his name were the words, "two times" followed by "butt-ass naked," three hand-drawn stars, six dates, and the name of a local high school.

I figured this was a list of men with whom the victim had engaged in sex, but to prove my suspicion, I would have to put her under oath and ask her. The trouble is, in most rape cases, because even a prostitute can be raped, the Rape Shield Statute prohibits the defense from inquiring into the victim's history of sexual escapades. I took advantage of an exception to the Rape Shield Statute by arguing that the statute didn't apply when questions of consent were at issue. I dreaded taking a sworn deposition from the young girl, where I would potentially have to take her through this traumatic recitation, but I had to prove that the "Incidents" document was what I thought it was. My client's future depended upon it.

As I suspected, the nine guys named on the "Incidents" list were high school boys with whom the victim had been intimate. When she wrote "6 times" next to Randy's name, it meant that she had had sex with him on six separate occasions. If a guy received four stars, like Michael did, that meant that the sex was outstanding. A boy who received no stars, like poor Tyrone, was "no good," she explained. She also said she wrote things like "butt-ass naked" to help her remember whether the encounter involved clothing. The dates, of course, were the dates on which she had had sex with the boy in question.

All the dates were clustered within one year. They led right up to my client's name and two dates. (In case you're wondering, he was given three stars, and they did it with their clothes on.) I tried to be as pleasant and professional as possible, but she wound up crying several times during the deposition. We were both relieved once her testimony was finished.

A few days later, I got a call from the prosecutor, informing me that the charges against my client were being dropped. I didn't bother asking why; I just thanked her. I'll probably never know with certainty why the prosecutor dropped the charges. Most likely it's because the "Incidents" list undermined her confidence in the victim's honesty, or maybe she knew it would be too difficult to win the case against my client with the "Incidents" list as evidence, and the victim facing another grueling examination in front of open court.

I was pleased I had decided to take the case. I chose to focus on thoughts that served me well. Judging the case and my client wouldn't have served me well at all, and if I had done so, my client could easily have been locked behind bars. Getting into the "business of is-ness" was key to such a positive outcome.

A Public Shaming

There must be some limits to this "is-ness" stuff. Surely, there must be scenarios to which this mindset will not apply. What if you woke up one morning only to learn that the night before, you had been publicly shamed on national television before millions of viewers? In such a unique scenario, aren't you allowed to call it "bad?" You're free to *label* it bad, but if your goal is to achieve happiness, that would not be the best choice.

This public humiliation scenario sounds far-fetched, but it happened to me. One morning when I first woke up, I was inundated with emails and text messages letting me know that English comedian, actor, and television host John Oliver had slain me on his HBO show, *Last Week Tonight*. Even my kids received texts.

Oliver's show revolved around the topic of "public shaming." During the segment, he played a *Fox News* clip in which I had provided comments about a woman who was suing her nephew after his enthusiastic hug caused her to fall and receive injuries. Oliver felt we were publicly shaming the aunt, who had provided a reasonable explanation as to why she had to name the nephew in the suit. During the clip, I joked by saying, "Hashtag worst aunt ever!"

After finishing my remarks, another "talking head" provided a witty response. I laughed on-air in a way that could understandably be described as forced, inauthentic, and obnoxious.

I must have subconsciously chosen to exaggerate my laugh to make the other guest feel better and make the segment more compelling. Also, at the time I made those remarks on *Fox News*, I had not been privy to the aunt's full explanation of why she sued her nephew.

Oliver seized the moment by, according to his own words, choosing to "publicly shame me." He stated that personalities like me are more interested in filling time than in telling the truth. *Ouch!* He then displayed photos of me, all pulled from the Internet. He called me a "human popped collar, whose every facial expression says I only wished the movie *Green Book* had won more Oscars." His audience laughed thunderously.

As I viewed the clip, I knew I had two options for how I could choose to feel:

Option #1: *I'm humiliated. This is horrible. People will think less of me. This will hurt my business. I'm ruined.*

This first option would not have served me well, so I went with option #2: *This is hilarious. I would have done the same thing if I were him. I can't wait to post this on social media and share the laughter with others.* I chose to believe that it just *is*. Instead of leaving it there, I kicked it up a notch and had fun with it.

I made the decision to take control of my feelings and only accept those thoughts that would serve me well. Did all those dreadful outcomes from option #1 actually take place? Nope!

Did I have way more fun than anyone being publicly humiliated is supposed to? Yup!

This SALADS stuff works. It can get you through anything if you apply it wholeheartedly.

Wish Your Enemy Well

How do we deal with people who keep doing us wrong — people who are nasty, rude, abusive, and obnoxious? How do we change our perspectives about those kinds of people? How can we choose happiness when it seems their goal is to ensure we experience the opposite?

One option is to keep doing what you've been doing. Continue to react the same way.

How's that working out for you?

Nothing will change until *you* change.

Make a decision to think differently toward those you think have done you wrong. I recommend a technique I call, "The Resentment Declaration," which goes something like this:

"I grant (insert the name of person who you've got issues with) everything I've ever wanted, everything I've ever needed, health, peace, and prosperity."

Why would you ever wish someone who has done you wrong well? Wishing your "enemies" well is the only way to achieve serenity because it releases the hold they have over you.

Martin Luther King once said, "Love is the only force capable of transforming an enemy into a friend."

While it may seem unnatural for you to wish people who have hurt you well, forgiveness is an essential part of once-and-for-all healing. Holding onto hurt only keeps causing you harm. "Holding onto bitterness is like swallowing poison and hoping the other person will die."[10] "Fake it until you make it." The process will feel awkward and forced as you'll be trying something new and getting out of your comfort zone. Practice it enough and it will work for you.

I got into the practice of reciting the Resentment Declaration before spending time with people I knew would create challenges for me. This strategy worked best with certain prosecutors or family members. By anticipating the way they might act and how they would make me feel, the declaration became a preemptive tool that helped me before I even stepped into the encounter. Wishing them well always changed my thoughts, which changed how I felt.

Has anyone ever done you wrong? The answer is, "Never!" You have never been wronged, because *feeling* wronged is just that, a feeling. Change your defensive thoughts to say, "No one has ever

---

10   Attributed to multiple sources. See https://www.quora.com/Who-said-the-phrase-Holding-a-grudge-is-like-drinking-poison-and-waiting-for-the-other-person-to-die

done anything wrong to me. Whatever they did, they just did. It was *my* reaction to what they did that dictated how I felt about it."

How things are perceived by you is completely in your hands. No one can feel your pain for you; no one can choose your thoughts for you. You are the only one in control of your experience. The moment you start seeing that your feelings dictate your thoughts will be the moment in which you become empowered to change them! Recognize the feeling. Embrace it. Recite the Resentment Declaration to release it — and the person you view as having harmed you — into the light.

Action Steps

1. Name your brain. Then, speak to your brain by using his/her name. Ask your brain to send you thoughts that serve you well.

2. Light it up! On a piece of paper, write down the thoughts that don't serve you well. Include your current fears. Then, (carefully and safely) light that piece of paper on fire. Take the ashes and bury them in your back yard under something visible (like a flower pot or small statue). Or collect the ashes in a baggie and keep them in a place you visit often (like the

area where you leave your keys or a part of your house that you visit often).

3. Write down a thought that has been troubling you. Then rewrite the troubling thought in a way that serves you well. (For example, change "I don't have enough money," to, "I have all the money I need for now.")

4. Best Wishes for Others. Think of one person who has been angering or irritating you. Say the following out loud, as often as you need: "I grant _____ (insert the name of person who you've got issues with) everything I've ever wanted, everything I've ever needed, health, peace, and prosperity." Repeat that several times and commit to saying it daily as often as needed.

Step 6: Smile!

We've made it to the final "S" in SALADS. Let's review the steps again:

The first action we take when we face unwanted emotions is to *stop*.

Then, we *arm ourselves*.

Next, we *look for the right spiritual tool*.

Then we *act*.

Afterward, we *decide* whether to be happy or not. Since few people would ever choose to be unhappy, the next and final step makes a lot of sense: Smile!

Do what you did when you were a toddler as long as you had your basic needs met — before mortgage payments, before stressful jobs, before thoughts that don't serve you well entered the picture. This was a magical, sweet, innocent time before fear, judgment, and guilt set in.

Return to that time and just smile. If you don't feel like it, fake it. No matter what you need to do for yourself, change your frown into a smile. Thanks to the happiness formula, your smile will arise naturally in due time, assuming it hasn't already. The old song says, "When you're smiling, the whole world smiles with you." Others respond to your energy. If they see you smiling, they are more apt to respond with the same expression.

Think back to my gummy bear experiment and how my expressive joy rubbed off on the officers in the deposition room. The energy you put out usually comes right back to you.

Action Steps

1. Smile. Hold that smile on your face for ten seconds. Repeat three times. Commit to doing that exercise daily for 90 days.

2. Go out in public and smile at at least three people — the more the merrier. Commit to doing that every day for the next 90 days.

Conclusion

There you have it. The key to your future health and well-being comes down to one word: "SALADS." Every time you
see any kind of salad — house, Greek, tuna, egg, fruit, potato,
taco, Caesar, Waldorf, macaroni, pasta, cobb, chicken or spin-
ach — think about how happiness is a *choice*. Salads will serve as
a reminder that you are the only one responsible for your happiness. Change your level of happiness by choosing thoughts
that serve you well.

How many times have you been in a restaurant when, immediately after placing your order, the waitress says, "That comes
with fries. Is that okay?"

Most people just say, "Sure" without thinking.

Fries are the default side dish that accompanies many restaurant orders. Rarely does your waiter say, "That comes with a
healthy green salad on the side. Are you okay with that?" To find
a healthier life, go against the grain and reject default selections
and tendencies. Refuse to let negativity, doubt, and hopelessness
slip into your psyche.

Speak up and take specific actions to obtain what's best for you, even if it's less delicious. The same applies to your thought processes. What comes from your brain by default are thoughts that don't serve you well — fries! To obtain the happiness you desire, request SALADS as often as possible. Transform your stinkin' thinkin' into thoughts that serve you well.

Abraham Lincoln once said, "We are as happy as we make up our minds to be." What was true over 130 years ago still rings true. You now have the formula for increasing your happiness as quickly as you want to. No matter how hard you try, your brain will send you thoughts that don't serve you well — and other barriers to happiness will pop up from time to time — but remain persistent. Fighting for your happiness is worth the effort.

All barriers that prevent you from making the decision to change your mind can be overcome. Money isn't an issue; it costs nothing to change your mind. In fact, if applied immediately and effectively, SALADS will *increase* your financial rewards.

What will people think of you? What people think of you is none of your business. Be prepared for friends, family, and others to strike up some judgment toward the "new you." Those around you are accustomed to seeing you act and think a certain way. Change is not always welcomed, and it can be unsettling — we all like a certain level of predictability — but as you evolve your